he loves

how to break
the cycle
of painful
relationships

I dedicate this book to my two
children, Jeshuah and Danah, who
I love and admire with all my heart.

Joanne Robinson

Lastword Publications
Lowestoft, Suffolk, UK
www.lastwordpublications.com

Copyright © Joanne Robinson 2010

The right of Joanne Robinson to be identified as author
of this work has been asserted by him in accordance with
the Copyright, Designs and Patents Act 1988.

First published 2010, by Lastword Publications
www.lastwordpublications.com
Lastword Publications works with authors and musicians,
businesses and charities to provide professional results
with maximum impact.

ISBN 978 0 9559439 2 8

All rights reserved.

No part of this publication may be reproduced, stored in
a retrieval system, or transmitted in any form or by any
means – electronic, mechanical, photocopy, recording, or
any other – except for brief quotations in printed reviews,
without the prior permission of the publisher.

Useful website links:
www.donnaintera.co.uk
www.loveinseason.net

Unless otherwise indicated, all Scripture quotations are taken from
the Holy Bible, New Living Translation, copyright © 1996. Used by
permission of Tyndale House Publishers, Inc., Wheaton, Illinois 60189

Design and production by The Upper Room 020 8406 1010

The Spirit of the Sovereign LORD is upon me,
because the LORD has appointed me
to bring good news to the poor.
He has sent me to comfort the brokenhearted
and to announce that captives will be released
and prisoners will be freed.
He has sent me to tell those who mourn
that the time of the LORD's favour has come,
and with it, the day of God's anger against their enemies.
To all who mourn in Israel,
he will give beauty for ashes,
joy instead of mourning,
praise instead of despair.

Isaiah 61: 1–3

Contents

A new start

Preface

The stories in this book are based on my real-life experiences of trying to find love in all the wrong places. After discovering God's love and seeing its life-changing results firsthand, I felt inspired to write about my journey for women who want to explore their relationships from a Christian faith perspective.

My desire is to communicate a message of hope for those of you who are despairing over your failed relationships. You may be searching for answers to the same questions I faced: Why do I keep picking the wrong guy? Why won't he change? Why won't he love me the way I want to be loved? You've been hurt before; you've been betrayed, lied to, cheated on, abused, or abandoned. Maybe you, too, have been left to cope with mounting debt or single-parenting. What you want more than anything in the world is for the next man to treat you right, settle down, and love you—but deep inside a part of you doesn't really believe that could be possible.

This book won't tell you how to secure a man's loyalty and devotion or help your man become 'Mr Right'. Instead, the messages in this book will show you why loving him is hurting you, give you hope that your life can change, and, most importantly, point you to the source of real love. If you open your heart to this new way of approaching life, you will discover a love that never dries up or goes cold. That might be hard to believe right now, but stick with me because it really is possible for you to know what it is to be truly loved.

I also hope that this book will help family and professionals understand some of the internal struggles women face when they love men who don't love them very well in return. Concerned outsiders often question why women stay in detrimental relationships, viewing their choices with bewilderment, confusion, and even judgement. What most women find helpful is having an advocate. They long to have someone beside them that can listen and look past their own frustrations, and help them to make sense of their confusion and fears.

Women who have read this book have told me they relate to my experiences and that the stories have been instrumental in helping them break free. Colleagues have used the reflections as a daily reading for their small groups. My hope is that this book will be a useful resource to you, whether you are building your own understanding of broken relationships, helping loved ones, or assisting clients in your practice.

Maintaining painful relationships and constantly worrying about a partner can drain a woman's emotional energy, leaving little mental stamina for long periods of concentration. I believe this is one of the reasons I was inspired to write short and very practical messages. You can choose to read from cover-to-cover or simply dip into subjects you feel are immediately helpful. The reflections and prayers at the end of each segment offer ways for you to personalise the principles that I learned. They are intended to help you gain power and strength from God, who desires to give you the freedom to live the life He designed for you.

Introduction

Lying awake before the frantic morning rush to get ready for work began, I would often roll to my left-hand side to see if my boyfriend was awake. Watching him sleep, I felt reassured: I had someone to share my life with; I was not alone. I was comforted to know that someone wanted me and loved me! We may have had a difficult and stressful relationship, but his physical presence beside me was a visible sign that he cared about me.

I needed this man in my life because I hated being alone. If my bed was empty, it meant he didn't care enough to be there in the morning. His absence only reinforced the idea that there was something wrong with me.

On a bright, crisp, autumn morning in London, I woke from a very sound and blissful sleep. As I stretched and turned, I realised I had little room to manoeuvre and, still half-asleep, it took a few moments for me to figure out why. I was lying on the left-hand side of my bed, the side once occupied by my boyfriend. As I rolled back and stared at the ceiling, the events of the previous night flashed through my mind. The man I had been living with for six years, the man at my left-hand side every morning, was gone. I had finally found the courage and strength to end our relationship. As I contemplated the evening's events in my half-empty bed, I became acutely aware that I did not feel alone! For the first time in my life, instead of waking up feeling empty, I woke up full of hope and joy! There may have been no man beside me, but I felt God's presence confirming that I belonged to Him and that He would always stand by me. Joy flowed from my heart – a heart touched by the love of God.

This joy was not founded in being free of another man. I still deeply cared about my boyfriend. We had been together a very long time and he was a huge part of my life, but our relationship had been laden with difficulty and I had begun to self-destruct. All of my relationships eventually turned out the same way. I had dated, been in long-term commitments, and even been married for a short while, but each break-up left me further in debt, less trusting of men, and further brokenhearted. Whether the relationship produced an abortion, betrayal, violence, or emotional abuse, I was left feeling devastated, with no strength left to start over. Yet despite my history with men, I was unable to put a stop to the behaviour that caused me to repeat the same mistakes over and over again.

I was in my early thirties before I knew what it was like to experience true joy and peace. I was raised in a family that had been living with abuse, loss, brokenheartedness, and deep disappointment for over three generations. At the tender age of ten, when my parents divorced, the legacy of abuse had not ended for me. The wounds had already destroyed my self-worth and confidence. I entered adolescence believing I was ugly and a failure. I believed that there was something very wrong and different about me.

No one knew what was going on inside, including myself. I had learned how to stop feeling in order to cope with the fear that permeated our home during my childhood, but my survival skills did not equip me to take care of my emotional needs. I didn't know what it felt like to be in a healthy relationship. When I started dating, I was guided by my negative experiences and my broken heart pulling me in every direction where I thought love might be waiting.

The stories in the first two sections of the book are based on my experiences between the ages of fourteen and thirty-two and are derived from my dating and long-term relationships, including a failed marriage. The men that I describe are not based on one particular lover, but instead represent the type of attitudes and behaviours I gravitated towards. By not focusing on specific individuals, I have tried to protect the identities of the men in my past, focusing each segment on my brokenness alone. The third section discusses some further lessons I gained while learning how to have healthy relationships. At the end of this book, I have included notes for those of you who might be interested in knowing how to spot early warning signs of an unhealthy relationship and characteristics of abuse.

If you have not experienced an abusive childhood or relationship, that does not mean you do not qualify to read this book. If you have read some of the reflection titles and identify, please read on. Not all of the stories are about abusive behaviour, but about choices that can lead to disappointments and unfulfilling relationships.

Whatever your experiences, my desire is that the Person and Life I discovered will be revealed to you, for it is God's ultimate purpose and plan for you to know the One who loves you most dearly and in the process become a whole and complete woman in Him.

Blame, lies and excuses

People soon become thirsty again after drinking this water. But the water I give them takes away thirst altogether. It becomes a perpetual spring within them, giving them eternal life. (John 4: 13–14)

The Samaritan woman may have thought her five broken marriages were a result of being unlucky in love, but Jesus helped her understand that the emptiness she felt inside would never be satisfied by seeking out a man to love her.

Until the Lord became the ultimate source of love in my life, I too went from one relationship to the next, looking for someone to make me whole. In the following devotionals, I share the blame, lies and excuses I accepted in an effort to gain love and the ways Jesus showed me what real love is all about.

Nice men are boring

Search me, O God, and know my heart; test me and know my thoughts. Point out anything in me that offends you, and lead me along the path of everlasting life. (Psalm 139: 23–24)

I remember a time when I believed that I could never meet a nice man, yet when I did meet one, I would view his strengths as weaknesses. It seemed that though I wanted a man that could treat me right, relating to him was another thing!

To me, dating the good guy felt too predictable. I wanted excitement and a challenge. I chose men that were aloof and unavailable or lived edgy, drama-filled lives. No rough or calloused exterior could deter my affections; there was something about each 'bad boy' that I found absolutely irristable.

Eventually, those 'cute' and 'challenging' traits would become the main points of contention of my relationships. The man that appeared strong and quiet only deepened my inner loneliness because he never shared his plans or thoughts with me. The man that was a challenge to tie down didn't want expectations placed on him, so I never knew where I stood. The man who wanted fun without commitment turned out to be a constant source of frustration and disruption to my plans.

God's word says that two people cannot walk together unless they agree *(Amos 3: 3)*. When I looked at my own life, I realised how much I had in common with these men that frustrated me so greatly. While a lack of commitment bothered me, I felt suffocated by the thought of a man wanting to be close to me. I easily slipped into the role of fixing things when my man didn't want to be responsible. Though I desired to be with a man who exercised self-control and faced problems boldly, I, like the men I dated, used alcohol and stimulants to ease emotional pain. I fit too well with the wrong type of man to be able to 'walk together' with anyone else!

If you want to have less in common with bad boys and be attracted to a man that will treat you right, ask the Holy Spirit to show you the deeper motivations behind your actions *(John 16: 8)*. Don't be afraid of facing the Holy Spirit's revelations or allowing Him to uncover the pain you have carried in your heart, for He speaks to you with love and not condemnation. He is your Comforter and Teacher. He is able to change your heart and remove the desires that lead you into unhealthy relationships.

The Holy Spirit will transform your thinking. With His help, you will begin to see that a man is not boring simply because he is reliable. You will no longer think a man is weak if he shares his feelings or say he lacks backbone if he doesn't walk with a bit of an attitude. You will be able to make distinctions—controlling demands for all of your time and attention will no longer be mistaken for true passionate attraction and a rebellious nature will no longer be able to masquerade itself as confidence and independence.

Ask God to reveal your patterns and work on changing these amongst safe people outside of romantic unions. As you grow used to drama–free relating, your tastes will change and you will start to be attracted to men who also share your values.

Reflection

Write an inventory of your significant relationships. What common characteristics do you see in the men you date? Are they critical, angry, or draining types? Do your romantic relationships remind you of other past relationships, including those with family members and friends? Do you find you respond to these people in the same ways, perhaps trying harder and harder to please them, waiting for them to change, or trying to win their affections? Do you find it difficult to be attracted to people who want to know you and love you on a deeper level because you haven't been given this kind of attention in the past? What relationship patterns have been revealed that you would like to bring to God for healing and change?

Prayer

Dear Lord, the broken hidden parts in me have often found something familiar in the hidden and broken parts of other people. Together, we have become more broken and hidden. Lord shine Your light in me; then I will see the things in my heart that keep me in darkness! Set me free Lord, so I can walk with You and be attracted to people who walk in the light with You!

He wouldn't say it if he didn't mean it!

Smooth words may hide a wicked heart, just as a pretty glaze covers a common clay pot. (Proverbs 26: 23)

During a girls' night out, conversation drifted to the subject of the new man in my life. We discovered that some of my friends knew him, and they advised me to be careful, as he had a reputation as a womaniser. Though their advice initially troubled me, I told myself that I could handle the situation. After all, just because he had a bad reputation in the past, that didn't mean he would be the same way with me. I paid no attention to their warning.

Though I was not aware of my feelings at the time, I desperately needed to know that I was wanted and desirable. I lived with a constant sense of insecurity; I feared no man would ever think I was good enough for him and that I would be unable to maintain a man's interest. I felt much better about myself with men who could charm away my fears and insecurities and easily trusted those who sought to flatter me.

While in the back of my mind I was determined to prove my friends wrong, I couldn't deny the evidence that my new boyfriend was being unfaithful, even though he would not admit it. I threatened to leave, but he always convinced me to stay. Confused, I reasoned that he wouldn't say he loved me if he didn't care about me. His behaviour proved his unfaithfulness, but his charm and persuasion kept me by his side. The more I listened to him, the harder it became to determine the right thing to do.

Women who are easily flattered by attention and promises of love often end up giving their love and trust too soon. If their lover turns out to be a charmer, they are overwhelmed with disappointment and find it hard to trust other men because of all the broken promises they've heard in the past. The Lord is eager to assist any woman who struggles in this way. The love Christ offers is abundant and prevents us from feeling starved for attention and affection. Satisfying yourself with God's love and being involved with a community of people who can love you for who you are will help you become used to feeling loved all the time. This kind of support will guard you against falling for a charmer's flattery and false promises of eternal commitment!

The Lord also wants us to learn new skills and look at people the way He does. He does not want us to be flattered by charm and smooth words or be impressed by money, position, or education. These things can hide a heart that has no love and cover traits such as deceit, unfaithfulness, selfishness, and jealousy. He wants us to learn to discern a man's character, because that is what we will live with on a day-to-day basis.

Instead of focusing on the things a man says, try to see the person he is underneath the smooth words and fine display. As you look deeper, you will start to recognise the attitudes and behaviours that have led you on in the past. Discuss these revelations with God and your community so that you can find strength to respond differently. As your behaviour changes, your hope in God's plan for your life, yourself, and relationships will light up again.

Reflection

Is your self-image based on the way God sees you or do you look for affirmation from others to know that you are desirable and wanted? Do you look for character or are you easily impressed by what a man says when you first meet him? Reflect on Psalm 101. What did David decide to do? What types of people did he avoid and what types did he seek out? What does his example teach you?

Prayer

Dear Lord, my need to feel desired, hear the words 'I love you', and be sweet-talked have often led me to fall in love with the wrong guy. Lord, I need to feel loved and wanted all the time, not just when a man is giving me attention! Fill my life with your love and give me wisdom and understanding so I don't fall victim to charm and flattery again.

He is my life

I pray that from his glorious, unlimited resources he will give you mighty inner strength through his Holy Spirit. And I pray that Christ will be more and more at home in your hearts as you trust in him. May your roots go down deep into the soil of God's marvelous love. (Ephesians 3: 16–17)

I was much more focused when I wasn't in a dating relationship. I kept to an exercise routine, ate healthily, developed a savings plan, pursued a career, and enjoyed family activities, but I found it hard to stay on track when I got tired of being single.

When I met someone new, I would quickly adapt my lifestyle until the only thing left on my agenda was him! It was not unusual for me to spend every spare moment with a new man, to the exclusion of my family and other interests. Forfeiting my personal agenda was easy because each relationship felt so exciting in the beginning, but over time my enthusiasm caused many problems.

As I chose to be so accommodating, I became offended when a man didn't always make the same personal sacrifices. I would resent his freedom and my jealousy, at times, could cause terrible arguments. I would wistfully remember how I once had a life, and how that life was on hold while I waited for a man to come home. My confidence would begin to plummet and I would start to feel depressed. Work would become a chore, and I would struggle to drag myself out of bed, to the office, or to see anyone. In one instance, I even gave up a career I loved and when the relationship ended, I realised just how much I had sacrificed.

Before I found God, I made relationships my only focus and, as a result, I lost my life over and over again. As I write these stories, I can now date without losing myself. Today, I am experiencing balance; I can enjoy the process of getting to know someone and yet busily maintain all the other areas of my life that are important to me.

So how did God transform my life so drastically? When I think about how I changed, I think of the word 'established'. When we say that something is established, we say that it has permanence; it had been securely set in place. That is what God did with me. He established my life by helping me deal with my intense loneliness and gave me friends I could trust and be myself with. He gave me a calling and a sense of meaning in my work. He gently drew me away from the lie that merging myself with another person would fill the emptiness inside of me.

God's love is unchanging and unfading and when you ground yourself in Him, you too will be established. He will give you the security you need in your heart and a sense of purpose that will keep you happy and focused on serving Him. You will recognise that the Lord has established this promise in you: *'Blessed is the man who trusts me, God, the woman who sticks with God. They're like trees replanted in Eden, putting down roots near the rivers—never a worry through the hottest of summers, never dropping a leaf, serene and calm through droughts, bearing fresh fruit every season' (Jeremiah 17: 7–8 MSG).*

Reflection

Are you grounded and established in the Lord as a single woman or have you found you are easily uprooted? What uproots you? Are you losing yourself because of your date's wishes or your desire to feel close to someone? This week, prayerfully meditate on your needs and ask God to fill the areas where you easily lose and merge yourself to another.

Prayer

Lord, I can only handle being single for so long before I start to feel that life is incomplete without someone to love me! Now that I recognise this pattern, I want to be established in Your love. Make me strong, solid, and secure in You so that whether I am dating or not, I remain focused on serving You and continuing in the path that You have set before me.

He loves me; he loves me not

Everyone can see how much he loves me. (Song of Songs 2: 4)

As young children, when my friends and I had a crush on a boy, we would pick petals off flowers singing 'He loves me; he loves me not.' We had a lot of fun teasing each other with the results! As childhood gave way to womanhood, I still spent much of my time trying to figure out whether men really liked me or not!

I found that most men had no trouble initially as they made the first move, but they would often lose steam and become passive in their pursuit. With others, relationships seemed to drag on with no real purpose; they didn't want to break up, but their actions showed little initiative or interest in me. In each case, I became confused as to how I should interpret what was going on.

Here are some personal experiences you might identify with:

- He makes excuses to stay away—he is always too busy to see you, regularly cancels at the last minute, or stands you up—but won't break up with you either.

- He doesn't mind sleeping with you or accepting a spare key, but he doesn't want a marital commitment.

- He says he needs his space and doesn't ring for days on end. He waits for you to call, then tells you he has missed you or goes on about his intentions to phone you and his reasons why he didn't.

- He says he only wants to be friends, but he carries on treating you like a girlfriend.

- He always forgets his commitments with you, but when you mention your concern, he feels attacked and hurt or accuses you of being controlling.

- Though you've been dating for a while and he tells you he is serious about you, he doesn't want you to meet his friends and family or doesn't like you calling him unless he asks you to.
- He doesn't mind you acting like a wife, even though he can't picture himself wanting marriage at any time.
- He feels entitled to loyalty and commitment from you, but has a different standard for the way he treats you.

A constant sense of uncertainty is not part of a stable and honest relationship. God created pursuit, desire, and commitment and wants us to interact with each other in straightforward and honest ways. Don't remain quiet when you are being treated in any of the ways listed above. God treats you with honesty and respect and says that you are a gift to a man *(Proverbs 18: 22; Ecclesiastes 9: 9)*. Reserve your heart for the man that follows God's example and won't keep you hanging on a string.

When a man truly loves you, you will not have to second-guess his feelings or dissect his behaviour for meaning; his intentions will be obvious. If he wants to be with you he will definitively let you know his position and pursue you for a relationship. You can play the petal game if you like, but real love is easy to identify.

Reflection

Are you constantly looking for signs and searching for evidence of attraction? Do you feel like you never know where you stand? Start learning to recognise how men think and behave when it comes to interest and attraction. If you see a pattern developing in your life, think about your reasons for wanting to stay with men that are unavailable or keep you waiting and wondering. Consider the appropriateness your own availability. Are you giving too much too soon or requiring too little in your relationships, making it easy for men to disrespect you?

Prayer

Dear Lord, I find myself chasing love, looking for signs and waiting for a man to want me. My search has caused me all sorts of pain and cost me many tears. I am tired of fighting for love. I come to You just as I am, asking You to show me why I am in this pattern and change the way I behave. Thank You for hearing my prayer and answering me.

If I say yes, he will love me

*Or don't you know that your body is the temple of the Holy Spirit,
who lives in you and was given to you by God? You do not belong
to yourself. (1 Corinthians 6: 19)*

I never used to be good at waiting for the things I wanted. In
my opinion, 'waiting' was another way of saying 'wasting time'.
My impatient attitude resulted in immense financial debt and
inspired one unfinished project after another.

I was also in a hurry to find the right man, and each time I started
a new relationship, I rushed in with my heart open wide. As
everything happened so quickly, I often approached sexual
involvement with haste, as well. I assumed physical intimacy
would create a deeper emotional connection and increase the
chances of us staying together. I also thought that if I said no to
sex, I was saying no to love and I feared each chance to find it
would be my last. This kind of reasoning never led to the love for
which I was searching. I may have had a man's attention for one
night, but I still had an empty heart in the morning—something
no man could fix.

Hastiness in each relationship birthed a premature intimacy
that neither one of us could handle. Sexual involvement
changed the dynamics between us and made me feel closer to
a man, even though I hardly knew him. As a result, I needed the
security of a commitment. When I began to cling to a man, his
feelings about me would change. In his eyes, I went from being
a carefree and fun person to being a mistrustful and jealous
woman. If a man confronted these changes in my demeanour,
his comments only added to my insecurity and made me hold
on to him all the more. My actions would push men away at
the time I needed reassurance the most, having made myself
so vulnerable through physical intimacy.

Sexual involvement creates a bond that the Bible refers to as *'becoming one' (Genesis 2: 24)*. This bond is a unique gift that God gives to couples who have pledged their commitment and love in marriage. He didn't intend this kind of intimacy for couples who are dating and don't yet know if they will ever make it to the altar.

I never realised how much I underestimated the value God has placed on me. We are holy and precious to our Lord, and when we sleep with our dates, we undervalue His estimation. In some respects, we leave our dates to form their own opinions about our worth if we never demonstrate God's estimation to them.

When I think about how marvellous we are in God's eyes, using our bodies to gain love seems redundant. We have a higher calling to use our *'whole body as a tool to do what is right for the glory of God' (Romans 6: 13)*. One of the ways we give glory to God is by adopting His view toward sexual purity. Instead of equating waiting with wasted time, God wants us to see that self-control brings great rewards. God can heal our empty hearts and fill them with His love. As we focus less on the physical aspects of a relationship, we create a more stable environment in which to get to know the other person and learn about areas in our own lives where we need to grow.

If a man becomes demanding or doesn't want to wait until marriage before becoming sexually involved, these attitudes indicate that he is not interested in sharing a deep commitment with you. A man's heart is not won by easy victories; waiting will give him motivation to work on winning your hand. Your actions will declare to your date that you agree with God when he says that you are worth waiting for, precious and holy in His sight.

Reflection

Do you find that sexual involvement is the one sure way you can feel wanted, desired, and loved? The Lord is the source of all your needs. What can you bring to Him for fulfilment that you will not find in another empty sexual experience? What fears do you have about abstaining from sexual intimacy while you focus on building relationships based on respect, love, and understanding? What evidence do you see in your life that invalidates your fears? How can you use this evidence to begin thinking in a new, balanced way that will help you move past your fears?

Prayer

Lord, I admit I have looked for love through sexual intimacy. Help me know in my heart that I am loved deeply by You and develop in me a desire to wait for marriage.

It feels so right being with him

And we wandered around Mount Seir for a long time.
(Deuteronomy 2: 1)

I couldn't believe how right it felt. We hadn't been dating that
long, but it seemed like we had been together for years. I was
sure my sense of comfort was a sign that he must be the one
for me. I gave my all and didn't look back.

In reality, this new relationship seemed familiar because it was
just like all the others I had been through before. Finally, at the
age of thirty-two, I began to see what I was doing! I realised
that though I had changed my address, my man, and my job,
I was still arguing about the same problems, feeling the same
frustrated feelings, and getting nowhere!

If you keep going 'round the same mountain', but with a
different man each time, it's time to make an emergency stop!
If you've grown accustomed to chaos and disappointment in
your relationships, pay close attention when something feels
strangely familiar with someone new. Don't see familiarity as
a green light to drive on; think about what is causing you to
feel so comfortable. You may have taken this route before!
Think back to your previous relationships and look for repeated
patterns. For example:

- When he starts shooting off and blowing his top, do you
  submit to or pacify his anger? Are angry and aggressive
  relationships familiar to you?

- Was he all over you initially, yet now that you are moving
  forward, he has become emotionally distant? Are you
  longingly waiting or fighting with him to connect with
  you? Have you felt alone in other relationships? How is that
  loneliness affecting this relationship?

- Are you taking the role of a parent? Is your man happy that he has met someone that can keep him in check? Does this mothering role make you feel good in some way? What were the costs of playing this role in previous relationships?
- Do you find yourself giving in, accepting all his wishes, and allowing him to take over? Does his control make you feel protected and wanted? Are you losing touch with your family and friends again? Has it become routine to put your life on hold and stop pursuing personal interests?
- What other traits might be familiar to you? Are they good or bad? How do these behaviours affect you, both positively and negatively? Are the patterns you've identified worth repeating?

When we walk with the Lord, He says He will bring new things into our lives, things not done before. The Lord desires to change your relational practices and give you an emotional connection you have never experienced. He will break the cycle! Listen to His promise: *'I will lead blind Israel down a new path, guiding them along an unfamiliar way. I will make the darkness bright before them and smooth out the road ahead of them. Yes, I will indeed do these things; I will not forsake them'* (Isaiah 42: 16).

Reflection

Repeating patterns with the same unfulfilling outcomes leads to hopelessness. Such repetition destroys the belief that things can ever be different and convinces you that a great relationship with someone can never be yours. Rather than putting your hope in your relationships, put your hope in God that He will fulfil His promise to lead you on a new path. As you open your ways to Him and learn how to do life His way, He will move you into new territory. Don't be afraid of change. Put your security in a God that never changes, as He will smooth the way ahead of you.

Prayer

Dear Lord, I submit myself to Your teaching. I want to grow in knowledge and understanding, not causing myself or others further pain. Please break the cycle of unhealthy relating in my life.

He is not like that with me!

*Don't let the errors of evil people lead you down the wrong path
and make you lose your balance. (2 Peter 3: 17 CEV)*

Bad company corrupts good character. (1 Corinthians 15: 33)

My date had a fantastic sense of humour. He liked to show me
off to his friends and take me out for a good time. He showered
me with gifts, bought me nice clothes, and knew how to make
me feel feminine and wanted.

My friends and family didn't quite share my perspective. They
saw another side of him—the person that got into trouble
with the law, who couldn't hold down a job and had a bit of
an attitude. I responded to their concerns by defending him.
I argued that they didn't know him like I did and that even
though he was having some trouble, I was willing help because
I believed I loved him.

I felt unaccepted and alienated because of my family's attitude.
I believed they were trying to push us apart for no good reason
and I was determined to remain loyal. I thought it was unfair and
unkind that they found fault with my choice in partner; I wished
they saw what I did and I wanted their support.

You can imagine the disappointment I felt when his problems
became mine. Though I had fun dating him, I was unrealistic in
my expectations that I would somehow be immune to what
my family and friends could see. I discovered that they had not
been judgmental or overly-critical; they just accepted things
that I didn't want to look at, for I feared the implications.

A healthy relationship requires learning to love without going
into denial about areas you fear to confront. If, like me, you find
that you blindly ignore a date's shortcomings, you are in danger

of settling for a kind of love that is not built on reality. God knows that if we don't gain an honest and realistic view of the person we are falling for, and confront behaviours and attitudes that are destructive, we run the risk of being hurt. For example:

The person who gains 'dishonest money brings grief to the whole family' (Proverbs 15: 27).

'A troublemaker plants seeds of strife' and 'gossip separates the best of friends' (Proverbs 16: 28).

'Violent people deceive their companions, leading them down a harmful path' (Proverbs 16: 29).

The hardest part of changing was facing my fears. I was afraid of confrontation and afraid of being on my own. I also believed I could not do any better. Jesus does not want us to be ruled by these kinds of fears. He has taught me that we should value ourselves enough to not settle for less than His best and have faith in His protection so that we can speak up.

When I learned that the Lord was always looking out for my best interests, I found it easier to let go of relationships that were not good for me. God wants your trust, too; He wants to help you gain the right perspective on what you are allowing into your life and confront it. Becoming a woman of truth will guide you on the right path every time.

Reflection

What problems have you been prepared to ignore in order to keep a relationship going? Are these things you need to confront and be honest about, rather than hope they won't affect you? God promises to meet all your needs (Philippians 4: 19). What assurance does this promise offer you when you face personal problems? (Please note, it would not be wise to confront somebody who would physically harm you in the process—seek help first).

Prayer

Dear Lord, I have oftentimes overlooked behaviour that was hurtful, thinking I could have a great relationship if I tried harder or ignored the problem. Help me to walk in the truth and fearlessly face up to the things I know are hurting me. Help me to speak the truth to myself and others without fearing loss because I have all I need in You.

He's not ready for commitment

The place where your treasure is, is the place you will most want to be, and end up being. (Matthew 6: 21 MSG)

Whenever I confronted my boyfriend's lack of involvement, he always replied, 'You know I love you, but I'm just not ready for a commitment.' One day when he repeated those words, I heard them differently. I didn't hear how much he loved me; I heard what he had been trying to tell me all along: He was not ready for a commitment. It finally dawned on me that I had given all I had to someone that did not want the same involvement that I desired.

Some women interpret mixed messages in the same way that I did: the word 'love' becomes the filter through which we hear everything else that is said. However, if a man says he is not ready for commitment, it's really important to listen to what he is saying. He is not ready. I know at times it seems easier to listen to what we want to hear rather than digest what is actually being said. We want to believe that eventually our man will commit, but as we withhold no part of ourselves from him, we give him no incentive to be more dedicated to us; he has already gained everything while giving nothing in return.

You will never experience the true companionship spoken of in *Ecclesiastes 4: 9–12* with a man that is not ready. This passage describes a partnership between two people who lift each other up when they fall, who comfort and protect each other in difficult circumstances. A man who isn't ready for commitment will not want to have this kind of involvement in your life; he will pull away from you and find reasons why he can't support you.

The Lord showed me a new way to respond to non-committal men. Though He loves the whole world and died to save us, only those who make the decision to commit to Him enjoy all the benefits of His presence *(1 Corinthians 6: 9–11)*. Adopt God's stance regarding distant people and only let the man that has made a marital commitment to you enjoy the benefits of marriage with you.

If you crumble at the thought of being more assertive, consider the reasons you are willing to settle for a one-sided relationship. God wants to give you abundant life *(John 10: 10)*. He wants you to be blessed while being a blessing to others. Don't feel guilty about pulling back or saying no instead of giving in. Setting boundaries will protect you, uncover his attitude towards your limits and show you how he really feels about you. No matter how things turn out, know that practicing God's way of doing things will give Him the opportunity to work out the results to your overall benefit *(Romans 8: 28)*.

Reflection

Have you wanted to be with your guy so much that you have given all of yourself to him? Have you hoped this personal sacrifice would motivate him to love you? What has it cost you to give without limits? Think about your reasons for giving your all to someone that is not interested in commitment, and work on setting boundaries.

Prayer

Dear Lord, I have given myself away, hoping to secure love and commitment from my romantic relationships. I am tired of giving too much and want to change. Teach me how to build strong relationships, based on mutual giving and receiving.

He's so confident and in control

And if it seems evil to you to serve the Lord, choose for yourselves this day whom you will serve. (Joshua 24: 15 NKJV)

I liked the way he took control of everything. It was nice to have someone make all the decisions for a change. He had a lot of confidence, which I admired, and it certainly allowed me to take the backseat and let him lead the relationship.

We didn't have many disagreements to begin with; he chose and I followed! I found his strong, almost forceful nature attractive and I interpreted his confidence as a sign of competence. When I started to feel a bit more comfortable in the relationship and began to do things for myself, I found my independence was met with resistance. If I didn't take his advice, he felt offended. I never felt heard, as his opinion always seemed to matter more than mine. He also showed a complete lack of trust. I could never spend a moment alone because he wanted to be with me all the time. If we didn't have plans for the night, he would make an excuse and turn up. If I resisted, I was accused of not caring enough about our relationship. Slowly, I gave up my preferences to maintain peace and avoid his inevitable retaliation.

I noticed a pattern in my life of attracting controlling people and as I prayed the Lord showed me where this pattern started. As a child I had no power to say no to living with emotional and physical abuse. I wanted my family to be at peace. I needed their love and the only way I could tolerate living as we did was to pretend that everything was fine. I learned to deny what was wrong and painful and try and make the best of my circumstances. It was an alien concept to think that people could truly respect, love, and listen to each other. I was saddened when

I realised that my early experiences had so greatly influenced my way of handling relationships as an adult.

Being found by God and being led by Him into a new life totally challenged my behaviours and beliefs. I learned that love neither abandons nor suffocates and it neither controls nor demands. It beautifully unites freedom and dependence upon others. The Father has shown me, through the example of Christ, how true love gives freedom:

Jesus never ignored hurtful behaviour in order to hold on to a relationship (Matthew 26: 17–25).

He spoke out against those who oppressed and controlled others (Matthew 23: 3–4).

He shared how He felt, but never threatened or bullied people to do things His way (Luke 13: 34).

He loved His family, friends, and disciples completely, but maintained His identity (Luke 2: 41–52).

He was powerful and mighty, yet He respected people's ability to make choices for themselves, even when they chose not to follow Him (John 6: 60–68).

The Lord wants you to distinguish between being controlled and being protected. If you are in a controlling relationship, address what is happening before it gets any worse or your man makes it difficult for you to leave. Remember, as you grow out of controlling relationships, you give real love a chance to show up, for *'love does not demand its own way'* (1 Corinthians 13: 5).

Reflection

Do you find it difficult to assert your opinions, views, and ideas? Do you have difficulty saying no? Is it easier to leave all of decisions to your partner? What has this cost you? How do you feel about saying no to those who treat you roughly? Though Jesus forgave and loved people very dearly, He also spoke out against those who threatened

Him harm (John 7: 17-26). How might Jesus' example encourage you not to feel guilty about confronting people in your relationships?

Prayer

Dear Lord, I am used to being seen and not heard. I would like to have a voice and to assert my views according to what You have taught me. Help me to not feel ashamed of making a stand and being a light in this world.

He didn't mean to hurt me

Behold, I cry out, Violence! but I am not heard; I cry aloud for help, but there is no justice. (Job 19: 7 AB)

There was a period during my childhood when I witnessed physical violence. Matters that were not dealt with eventually erupted into an explosion of anger and rage. Even after such episodes, the issues were not resolved and were put under the carpet until the next family conflict erupted into fighting and arguing again.

What I experienced had a profound effect on how I handled my relationships. I grew up to be a fearful person and gravitated toward emotionally cold men who disapproved of me. As I was desensitised to aggression, I had no power to assert myself when I was being mistreated. Anger had become a familiar acquaintance, and in spite of my fear, I grew accustomed to being in argumentative and aggressive relationships.

When God began His healing work in my life, I started to see that my version of love was very different from the real thing. A man that loves will approach problems with a desire to calmly work them out. He will not attack a woman to avoid disagreement. He will take responsibility for his actions and will cherish rather than harm. Even our Mighty God, as powerful and awesome as He is, treats His creation with tenderness: 'He will be gentle—he will not shout or raise his voice in public. He will not crush those who are weak or quench the smallest hope. He will bring full justice to all those who have been wronged' *(Isaiah 42: 2–3)*.

The Lord changed my perception of and response toward violence, and I no longer experience it in my life. He delivered me from the hands of the aggressor. He will set you free, protect you, build you up, and ensure that violence no longer enters your life, as well *(Isaiah 60: 18).*

You might be thinking that these promises sound good, but find it difficult to believe they will be fulfilled in your circumstances, especially if you are the victim of severe and life-threatening attacks. I want you to understand that there is no situation you will ever go through that is out of God's control. The Lord manages the entire universe and the stars; He sustains life and yet He is aware when the smallest bird falls to the ground. How much more, then, is the Lord concerned about what you go through on a daily basis? The Lord hates violence *(Isaiah 61: 8)* and will not leave you defenceless. Commit your situation to Him, for He will make a way of escape, even when you think that there is no way out.

In God's new kingdom, there is no place for people who have murderous and hateful hearts, a group which I believe includes violent and abusive people *(Revelation 21: 8)*. Yet the Lord's promises of peace are not for some future date. God's kingdom starts in your heart *(Luke 17: 21)*. Salvation belongs to you today. Do not be afraid; it's okay to feel weak and helpless because that is when God's strength works best. Trust that He will take your difficulties and make them work in your favour.

Start by breathing a prayer for God's protection. Seek out people who will pray and support you; take action to protect yourself and your family. Be courageous, and accept the help and support that comes your way. Trust God to bring you deliverance, and when He does, do not run back to your aggressor out of fear. Hold on to God's word because He will fulfil His promise if you trust Him: *'My people will live in safety, quietly at home. They will be at rest' (Isaiah 32: 18).*

Reflection

Are you in a threatening or violent relationship and living in fear? You may be blaming yourself or reasoning away your

man's lack of self control, but your excuses, love, patience, and understanding will not help him change. Rather, your toleration will expose you to further, escalated attacks. Violence is not an act of love; seek help and support to get out and remember that God will not leave you helpless and alone.

Prayer

Dear Lord, You are more powerful than people and I put my trust in You. Though I am afraid, there is safety in Your Name. I trust You to make a way out for me and end the violence in my life. You are my God and my Deliverer.

He doesn't treat me that badly

As for me, I am poor and needy, but the Lord is thinking about me right now. (Psalm 40: 17)

Late one night while I was home alone, I heard a knock at my door. I could hear the sounds of giggles and whispers. When I went to answer the door, I found my neighbours holding out my boyfriend's jacket. Trying not to laugh, they told me that my man had left the coat at one of their girlfriend's flats. They were trying to tell me that my boyfriend was being unfaithful without actually telling me. I felt too afraid to hear any more, and I didn't ask any questions. I simply took the jacket, quietly closed the door, and never said a word to my man about their visit.

My lack of response to the news of my man's unfaithfulness showed just how down-trodden I had become. For many years my feelings were numb and I didn't seem to experience any emotion, good or bad, in response to things that happened to me. That is why I did not respond to my neighbours' spiteful behaviour or confront what my man was doing behind my back. On several occasions, I didn't notice how badly I was being treated until someone pointed it out, amazed that I put up with such treatment.

Some time later, when I was no longer with this man, I asked him why he had treated me so badly. His response was, 'Why walk all over you when I can lie all over you?' In other words, 'Why take advantage of you slightly, when I can take advantage of you completely?'

In the book of Isaiah, God makes this promise to those who feel down-trodden: *'Therefore please hear this, you afflicted... See, I have taken out of your hand, the cup of trembling...You shall no longer drink it. But I will put it into the hand of those who afflict you,*

*who have said to you, "Lie down, that we may walk over you." And
you have laid your body like the ground, and as the street, for those
who walk over' (Isaiah 51: 21–24 NKJV).*

When God showed me this verse, I cried. It was as if He was
saying that He had heard what my ex-lover said to me all those
years ago and knew how crushed I felt. I felt such a release
because deep within I knew He was telling me those days
were over. Furthermore, He promised that He would change
my frailty to strength: *'Do you feel like a lowly worm, Jacob? Don't
be afraid. Feel like a fragile insect, Israel? I'll help you. I, God, want
to reassure you. The God who buys you back, The Holy of Israel,
I'm transforming you from worm to harrow, from insect to iron.
As a sharp-toothed harrow you'll smooth out the mountains, turn
those tough old hills into loamy soil. You'll open the rough ground
to the weather, to the blasts of sun and wind and rain. But you'll be
confident and exuberant, expansive in The Holy of Israel!' (Isaiah 41:
15–17 MSG).*

If you feel numb and find yourself excusing those who mistreat
you or have come to realise how much people walk over you,
let this promise of God be your hope that He will end those
days. He will lift you up so that you are no longer a doormat
and He will give you a heart, warm and tender, that can feel
again and give you boldness to face problems you once
considered too powerful and difficult to overcome.

Reflection

Have you felt that others take advantage of you? Talk to God
about what has happened and give yourself permission to
talk about how you really feel. Allow Him to begin fulfilling
His promises to help you stand up. Seek out supportive
friends and ask them to help you work through the
problems you find too difficult to face by yourself. Consider
learning new life skills to help you overcome feeling fragile
and vulnerable. What opportunities or courses are available

at your local church/college that will encourage you to have a voice, express your opinions, and develop your communication skills?

Prayer

Dear Lord, I have no idea how to face my problems. I am overwhelmed; they hurt too much and I can't do it alone. I need help. Lead me to the right people who can support me as I learn to stand up in You. Comfort me Lord, so I can come to You and start to open up. I need You.

He always comes back sorry

*So why does this people go backward, and just keep on going
– backward! They stubbornly hold on to their illusions, refuse to
change direction. (Jeremiah 8: 5 MSG)*

The break-up wasn't a pretty spectacle; actually I was very mad
at him and vowed I would never take him back. As time went
by, I started to miss him and, as if sensing my softening, he
called to see how I was doing.

He told me he was sorry for what happened and that life
wasn't the same without me. He was miserable and wanted me
back. The more I listened to his reasoning, the more I became
convinced that it wouldn't hurt to try again. I believed he had
truly changed and that the phone call alone proved he still
loved me. What had happened between us before seemed
excusable, even insignificant compared to the hope of a
second chance. I agreed to try again…and, of course, it wasn't
long before we were breaking up again over the same issues!

The first time he came back he wasn't sure how I would
respond. After that, I was predictable; he knew if he apologised
enough I would always take him back. With each request
for reconciliation, I asked myself the same questions: Had he
changed? Would our relationship be different this time?

In order to find answers, I needed to ignore my boyfriend's
readiness for a relationship and, with God's help, evaluate my
own emotional maturity and ask myself some tough questions.
What was causing me to keep taking my boyfriend back when
I had been disrespected and treated so badly? Was I willing
to give up my way of dealing with problems and follow God
in the matter? Would I seek wisdom and learn about healthy
relationships so I could be honest with myself and take

responsibility for my own weaknesses? Would I wait on God so that I could know the right course of action to take?

Coming to God in this way would have given Him the opportunity to change my thinking about my situation and help me stop the madness of continual make-ups and break-ups. This kind of change is something the Bible calls 'repentance'. It is a gift from God, not something we can achieve by ourselves *(Romans 2: 4)*. We experience repentance when we seek God to help us become more like Him. Without this kind of heart change, I could only expect my responses to carry on as they did before.

When my boyfriend apologised, I really hoped that he meant it, even though deep down I had my fears about how long his change would last. Accepting his apology alone was not sufficient. Part of my growth process required that I become more independent and wait patiently to see if he was committing himself to a path of growth and change, the same path God wanted for me.

You see, some people say they are sorry because they miss what they had. They do a few things differently for a while, but they don't maintain any lasting change. What you need to look for are signs that a man is taking responsibility for his actions without making excuses or blaming you for his faults. He needs to show you, over a period of time, that he has become a responsible and accountable person.

If he doesn't commit to this path, then it is pointless to expect that your relationship will be different in the future. Do not slip into denial and think there is something else you can do to fix it. God wants you to stay honest about your situation even if the outcome proves to be painful and disappointing.

The Lord's principles for working out difficulties can be trusted. If you allow Him to guide you and show you how to apply His truths, you will know what you need to do when your ex comes knocking at your door again. God will never leave you to figure things out alone, for He has promised to stick by your side and give you everything you need to be successful in life. He is willing and able to help you work out the problems in your relationships.

Reflection

Does your relationship consist of numerous make-ups and break-ups? What issues cause the break-ups? 'Red flag' issues such as addiction, hitting, lying, cheating, controlling, and obsessive behaviours are things you should not accept back into your life. Do you break-up over things that you can't live with, but are not necessarily fatal flaws? Things such as impatience, pushiness, and nagging can be worked through if the other person is owning their behaviour and working through repentance. Are there areas of your life you would like to turn around, seeking a path of change and growth?

Prayer

Dear Lord, I have been doing this for so long, waiting for him to change and hoping he means it this time. I now see that I can break out of this cycle by focusing on the changes needed in my heart first. Lead me on the right path. I need You because I handle problems in predictable and repetitive ways. Please grant me repentance and forgiveness as I don't want to keep making the same mistakes in love. Thank You for listening to me and answering me.

Waiting for him to change

Real life comes by feeding on every word of the Lord.
(Deuteronomy 8: 3)

I spent all day thinking about what I was going to say to him when he came through the door. I had all my reasons and justifications carefully rehearsed, but as soon as I saw him, all my resolve to stand up to him left me.

I found myself making excuses for what had happened. He seemed to be in a good mood and I really didn't want to face another upset. I hoped that if I tried to maintain peace and did my best it would be enough to change things between us.

I tried many tactics to encourage my boyfriend to be a better man. I treated him with exaggerated kindness and thoughtfulness. I tried to become exactly the kind of woman I thought he wanted. I made a point of forgiving him and putting all past wrongs behind me; I hoped to show him how tender and loving I was in an effort to encourage him to act in similar ways. I stressed the importance of keeping our family together. I even developed a plan to lose a few pounds, assert my independence, and get on with my life, just to see if I could make him come running after me.

No matter what I said, how many times I chose to keep silent, how long I waited and greatly I hoped, he never changed into the man I wanted him to be.

I didn't choose men who were fine just as they were. I chose bad boys and tried to make them good men. I didn't choose men who knew how to treat a woman right. I chose men who treated women badly and then tried to teach them how to treat women correctly. I chose men who told me they didn't want a serious relationship and then tried to make them be serious about me. I didn't choose men who were satisfied with me. I chose men who were easily distracted or wished that I looked different and then tried to be what they wanted.

I tried to fix men who didn't want to be fixed. I chose to keep them when they told me they knew they were treating me badly. I chose to wait for them to change when they told me they were content with their lives.

Finally, I realised that my problems with men kept following me around as a result of the choices I was making. I kept waiting for someone to transform into my ideal man because I thought being with the perfect person would make me happy. In essence, I was making each boyfriend responsible for my personal happiness and well-being. When I realised what I was doing, I decided to stop trying to change others and asked God to help me.

God heard my prayer and my life started to change. He showed me that the contentment and happiness I desired could only be found in Him, for He is the one who created me for His good pleasure and purposes. He showed me that only He could change another person, so I gave up trying to control others and became responsible for my own happiness and the direction my life was taking. As I focused on my own salvation, my interaction with others changed and that influenced how they treated me. Now I enjoy the type of relationships I have always wanted. I am no longer waiting, but living.

Reflection

Are you waiting for a man to change so that you can feel alive and loved by him? Do you keep picking unsuitable partners and hoping things will work out? How are these patterns affecting your life? What choices have they led you to make? Are you discovering more of the life God has for you or are waiting to enjoy life because you are waiting for your date to change? What do you need to take responsibility for instead of waiting for someone else to do it for you?

Prayer

Dear Lord, I thought it if I waited long enough, my man would eventually change and make me happy. I now see that I have been making him responsible for my happiness. I know now that I can experience happiness and fulfilment by abiding in You and focusing on what you want me to do with my life. Change my focus, Lord, so I can live in freedom.

Now I have his child

Surely now my husband will feel affection for me, since I have given him three sons! (Genesis 29: 34)

I have given much thought to the biblical story of Leah and the experiences she had as a wife and mother *(Genesis 29: 16–35)*. Leah had a younger sister, Rachel, who was very beautiful and a man named Jacob fell deeply in love with her. Custom in those times required that the eldest daughter marry first, so her father, Laban, tricked Jacob into marrying Leah before giving him Rachel's hand.

It was hard for Leah to be with a man who did not love her, but she hoped that by having his children she might change his feelings. Leah bore four children before she accepted the fact that childbearing could not win the affections of her husband. Instead she turned her attention to the Lord, and praised Him for the gift of her children.

Like Leah, I thought having a child would change my man's attitude, help him settle down, and encourage him to take up his responsibilities. I hoped to win his love and respect as we became not just a couple, but a family. Though he did calm down for a season, it wasn't long before he was living like a single man again. Ultimately, my situation didn't end as I had hoped. I became a single parent and made mistakes raising my kids. I dated when I wasn't healthy enough to make good choices and taught my children wrong things about love in the process.

Most of the time, I felt as if I did not have enough of myself to give to my children. It is so easy to feel overwhelmed as we try to hold everything together, especially if the father is being unsupportive or has deserted his family. When Jesus became a part of my family, we found hope. Great change and healing has taken place in all of our lives. I can look back and see that God's hand has led us through and wrought many miracles.

The Lord has always taken care of us and He will do the same for you; you have not been left without a helper. The Lord has a very special concern for the fatherless and speaks many times in His word about His promises of protection. He is called the 'Father to the fatherless' and the 'defender of widows' (Psalm 68: 5). The Lord has committed Himself to you like a husband and as a father to your children. He has a good plan for your future, so don't give up or give in to bitterness or despair, wondering how you are going to make it!

Don't be afraid of the journey ahead of you. Join forces with God and be hopeful, for He has great surprises in store. God has a great plan for you and your little one, and may even use your example to influence your child's father. Even if your children are teenagers or adults, it is not too late to see God work in your lives. Don't underestimate your Saviour, the power of prayer, or the impact of being a living testimony of how God has changed you.

If you are a single parent and have considered dating again, avoid choosing a man based on the belief that no one else would want you now that you have children. This idea is rooted in fear and has absolutely no truth in it. If you continue to believe this lie you will choose any man rather than have no man at all. Bring your worries to God for healing and let this life experience teach you how to rely on and be loved by Him; He has promised you that everything is going to be okay. Claim this promise: *'They will not work in vain, and their children will not be doomed to misfortune. For they are people blessed by the Lord, and their children, too, will be blessed. I will answer them before they even call to me. While they are still talking to me about their needs, I will go ahead and answer their prayers'* (Isaiah 65: 23–24).

Reflection

Having a baby cannot secure your man's love or make you
feel better about yourself. Children are not the antidote to
fix broken people or relationships. If you are a single parent,
set your course. You are a woman of purpose with a mission
in life, raising children of strong character. Live in God's
strength and do not cater to your weaknesses. Move forward
with hope; don't focus on past mistakes and failures. Your
children need to see your faith in action so they can grow up
with a sense of hope and purpose, too.

Prayer

*Dear Lord, I have thought about having a baby for many reasons:
I need to feel loved; I am lost and lonely; I want to hold on to my
man; I want to fix my relationship. I now see that having a child
won't give me what I hope to gain. Please forgive me. Help me
accept that I don't have the things I hoped for with this man.
I release my anger, jealousy, pain, and bitterness into Your hands.
Instead of seeking fulfilment by having a child, I accept the plans
and purposes You have for me.*

Prayer for Mothers

*Dear Lord, now that I have this child, help me to accept the reality
that the things I hoped would result have not happened. I release
any resentment I have toward the father of my child. Help me be
the best parent I can be and raise godly children for Your glory.
Fill my heart and restore my sense of worth so that I am not
tempted to think I am undesirable. Help me not to settle for a man
that is not part of Your purposes for me.*

He controls our money

The Lord replies, 'I have seen violence done to the helpless, and I have heard the groans of the poor. Now I will rise up to rescue them, as they have longed for me to do.' (Psalm 12: 5)

Waking early one morning, I caught my partner stealing money from my purse. When he realised I was stirring, he quickly put the money back and I pretended not to see, lying very still until he left the room. On other occasions he would lie and say he had paid our bills or he would pretend we did not receive a Social Security payment, which meant I had no means to pay for our provisions. I knew deep inside he was lying, but I was too afraid to say anything. On one occasion, in an effort to purchase an item I badly needed, I saved money without his knowledge. When he asked how I was able to afford the item, he replied I was right for hiding the money, because he would have spent it on himself. He showed no remorse for his attitude, but rather treated his behaviour as if it was his right to be that way.

Financial control can develop in different ways. It can stem from someone preventing you from working or furthering your education, refusing to share financial information, or pushing you to give up some form of financial independence you have previously enjoyed. Boundaries are constantly tested and pushed back until one person gains control over another through money.

If a guy you are dating pushes you for financial dependence on him, he could be seeking to create a situation in which you become reliant on him for your needs. Women who have gone down this road have been left feeling trapped and controlled. Resolve to date without giving up your financial independence.

If you are currently in a financially debilitating relationship, don't despair. Your faith in God can set you free. God's resources are not subject to the world's economy or the controlling behaviour of others. God is on your side and wants to free you from every type of oppression. Remind yourself that God has promised that *'even in famine [you] will have more than enough' (Psalm 37: 19)*. Believe this promise even when your circumstances look bleak. Christ has overcome every type of evil and oppression in the world. His power will loose the monetary shackles that bind you to this relationship and He will cause you to stand free in this area again.

Reflection

One of the earliest signs of future abuse is financial control. Bring your relationship into the light by speaking to someone who specialises in abusive relationships. Find friends who can give you emotional and spiritual support. Depending on your circumstances, you may need professional and legal advice. What services are available in your local community that can offer you guidance and direction?

Prayer

I remind You, Lord, of your promise to protect me and deliver me from every kind of oppression. I commit my financial affairs to You and I trust that You will make a way out of financial control. I am depending on You, Lord, and will follow Your way to freedom.

I can't focus on anything else!

Give all your worries and cares to God, for he cares about what happens to you. (1 Peter 5: 7)

There was a time when I was constantly worried about what was going on in my boyfriend's mind. He was involved in my life, but I never knew what he was really thinking and feeling about our relationship or our problems.

Though I went through the motions, taking care of my home and my family, I was never able to focus on spending much quality time with my children. I couldn't take my thoughts off my man long enough to rest and find peace in my daily life. When I spent time with friends and family, I couldn't seem to talk about anything other than my problems and worries with my man.

Anxiety and worry go hand-in-hand with unsafe relationships because they indicate a lack of honesty, security, and commitment between the couple. The Lord sees how greatly you worry and wants you to cast your cares on Him. He knows that when we lack wisdom and understanding, we don't have the knowledge to make informed decisions. We become consumed by paranoia, anxiety, and fear. The Lord says, *'My people are destroyed for lack of knowledge' (Hosea 4: 6 KJV)*. He wants us to focus on His word so His wisdom and knowledge can shine on our problems. *'The Lord grants wisdom!… He grants a treasure of good sense to the godly… You will understand what is right, just, and fair, and you will know how to find the right course of action every time… Wisdom will save you from evil people, from those whose speech is corrupt' (Proverbs 2: 6–12)*.

If you are constantly confused about your relationship, start asking God for answers. His wisdom will soothe your anxiety and bring you peace of mind. By being teachable and open to receiving instruction, you allow God to show you what to do and give you the boldness you need to step forward, assured that He is by your side. Leave tomorrow in His hands and focus on today, for He says to you, *'Don't worry about having enough food or drink or clothing…. Your heavenly Father already knows all your needs, and he will give you all you need from day to day if you live for him and make the Kingdom of God your primary concern'* (Matthew 6: 31–33).

Reflection

What are you worrying about today? Does worry ever solve your problems? Can it add to your life? What problems can you give to God to sort out for you? Worry makes us wish we knew the future. According to *Matthew 6: 34*, what does God want us to do?

God has given us the Bible and a host of relationship resources (i.e. counsellors, coaches, church ministries, books, DVDs and CDs) to help us grow in wisdom, so that we might not be overcome by our anxieties. What resources can you invest in today? Who can you turn to for help?

Prayer

Dear Lord, I give You my worries about _____. I choose to focus on Your promises and let You lead me through this day, moment by moment. Give me understanding so that I can apply wisdom to my problems. Remind me of ways You've helped me in the past so I will know deep in my heart that You will help me through this situation in my life right now.

I want the person he used to be back!

But when the Holy Spirit controls our lives, he will produce this kind of fruit in us: love, joy, peace, patience, kindness, goodness, faithfulness, gentleness, and self-control. (Galatians 5: 22–23)

The relationship started off with great possibilities. My friends would remind my new man how lucky he was to be with me and I believed I was lucky to have him! When he started to withdraw and become distant, no one could understand why he had changed so much, least of all me.

The problems began when he stopped following through on his promises to call me or return my calls. He started to find excuses not to come round and when we did make plans, he would show up late, or worse, not at all. I found myself anxiously waiting at home just in case he decided to turn up. I found it hard to concentrate on anything and I gradually started to put my life on hold for those few moments when he made himself available to me.

I felt completely alone and abandoned. I loved this man, but I hated the loneliness our relationship brought. I kept thinking about the good times and tried to make sense of why things had gone so wrong. I kept wondering what I had said or done to cause this change in him. I was equally disturbed when he did make an appearance and carried on like nothing had changed between us.

When I pointed out that he wasn't the same, he said there was nothing wrong. He accused me of being paranoid or said I didn't understand him or his needs. I would back off, thinking that would make him warm towards me again, and tried not to ask too many questions. The last thing I wanted to do was give him another excuse to leave.

All the while, my mind raced with questions. Why did he treat me this way? Why didn't he want to spend more time with me? Did he still want me? Why did he still show up if he didn't? Why couldn't he be like he was when we first met?

I felt so confused. He seemed to want me around, but only on his terms. I felt trapped in a miserable relationship, full of waiting and hoping. Then the rumours started—he was out having fun, partying, seeing friends, and hanging out with other girls. I wanted to confront him, but I had no idea where to find him. When he finally showed up and I questioned him about the things I had heard, he would get so angry that he would threaten to stay away even longer or simply say that he wanted to be left alone, to eat, to watch television – anything but talk to me.

When he left after one such episode, I knew I could not take much more, but something inside of me didn't want to let go. I wanted him; I thought I needed him and that I could never find someone who could make me feel the way he did during the early days of our relationship. I decided to wait in the hope that he would come back to me again.

Perhaps you have experienced a relationship similar to mine. You remember how your man was when you first fell in love and can't understand why he has changed. You desire the 'old man' back, but don't know what it will take for him to return.

If he is not like the person you first met, it is likely he portrayed an image of himself to impress you while you were getting to know each other. Eventually, the need to impress wore off and he started to be himself with you. This is the person you are with now. What have you come to know about him? Jesus said that you can know someone by the kind of fruit they produce in their life *(Matthew 7: 20)*. Is he showing the fruits of a godly character or has he brought pain and destruction with him? *Proverbs 18: 3 says: 'When the wicked arrive, contempt, shame, and disgrace are sure to follow'.* Look at what has 'followed' this man into your life since you have been in a relationship with him.

While you think on these things, also consider what you miss most about the beginning of your relationship with this guy? What do you continually reminisce about? Did you know that the Lord is able provide what you are missing? Prove His promise today for His word says *'Open your mouth and taste, open your eyes and see how good God is. Blessed are you who run to him. Worship God if you want the best; worship opens doors to all his goodness.' (Psalm 34: 8-9 MSG).*

Reflection

What help do you require from the Lord to help you stop yearning for the past and instead focus on how your relationship is affecting you today?

Prayer

Dear Lord, I have put my hope in my man, thinking back to how he used to be. What we had in the beginning is no longer there, but I keep waiting and hoping no matter how bad things get. I can't believe how different things are now, but I don't want to keep waiting just for a few moments of good times. I want to feel good every day and I know that starts by bringing myself to you and seeking a new way forward through prayer and listening for you to give me a new direction.

He loves me more than her

Loyalty makes a person attractive. (Proverbs 19: 22)

When the phone rang, the last person I expected to hear on the other end of the line was the woman for whom my boyfriend had left me. She called in a panic, having heard rumours that he wanted me back. I was not aware of his intentions, but the call left me with a sense of expectancy. A few weeks later, he contacted me. I was happy to accept his apology and give him a second chance.

However, things were not as they were before we split up and I was further dismayed when I discovered he was still dating the other woman. Though I argued and fought with my boyfriend, I blamed this woman for all our problems. She prevented my man from being with me. She wouldn't let him go and was insanely jealous. She didn't have a life. She had some wicked hold over my boyfriend and was making my life hell. She treated him terribly and was using whomever she could against him. Most importantly, I believed she was stopping us from being happy!

I was so busy fighting for my boyfriend that I lost track of the facts. He was unfaithful, but I had difficulty accepting the reality of his dishonesty. I allowed his charming personality and the fun we had together to blind me to his deceit. Unfaithfulness didn't fit my ideal of the man that told me he loved me, so I held on to him and denied what was really going on.

Perhaps you find yourself in similar circumstances. You are so focused on holding on that you haven't given yourself a chance to see the reality of your situation. You love your man and hope that he will choose you, but there is no special brand of feminine love that can magically cure an unfaithful heart. He has shown enough evidence of his true feelings. Consider why being without him is more difficult than sharing him. Chances are your desire to hold on isn't rooted in love, but in fear.

The Lord loves and cherishes you. He wants to change you into a woman that will not settle for a man who is unfaithful to you. He wants you to live in the light of His truth according to His values, because He knows you need more than feelings to make the right choices in relationships. Allow the Lord to show you the true nature of love, for it does not play games with the heart. Love is protective. Love will not lie to you. Love is kind and will always desire to build you up and esteem you. Love is faithful, and a man that loves you will not be interested in dividing his attentions with someone else.

God wants to help you make good choices and does not want you to experience the pain of building a relationship with someone who enjoys dating multiple women at the same time. As you choose not to fight for a man's loyalty, you will see that you are not losing someone's love, but are instead winning a victory over another person's unfaithfulness. When you resolve to make dating choices based on character, you will develop the power to say no to dishonest and unfaithful men. As you make better choices, you will have more opportunities to build relationships with those who share your convictions.

Reflection

Successful relationships are built on trust and loyalty, but are you settling for less? What are your reasons for settling? What damage caused by disloyalty and betrayal can you bring to God this week for healing? What do you think are the most important and meaningful qualities in a relationship? What would these qualities look like in action in your own life? This week, pray for the Lord to help you make the values you identified a part of your everyday life.

Prayer

Dear Lord, I have compromised with unfaithfulness and reaped only pain and heartache. I make the decision to no longer be a participant in deceitfulness by being unfaithful in my relationships or staying with unfaithful men. I desire to follow You and be like You. Please instil in my heart Your principles of love, loyalty, and honesty.

A new love will make me feel better

I want you to promise, O women of Jerusalem, not to awaken love until the time is right. (Song of Songs 8: 4)

After a relationship ended, I felt empty and lost. I couldn't wait to get out and start meeting other guys. It never occurred to me that the rush to find someone new was fuelled by the need to silence my pain.

I would have much preferred to take out an insurance policy against damages incurred in dating rather than take time out to heal. I wanted love and attention, not pain; but eventually running from one relationship to the next caught up with me. Just as it is unnatural to grow roses in the middle of winter or see snow fall in the middle of a heat wave, it is also unnatural to try to cultivate love while dealing with the loss of it. The Shulamite woman understood this when she said there was a time for love, a time when it would awaken. She warned that we should not try and wake love up before it is ready. Like the fertile soil that allows a plant to grow, we need fertile hearts for love to blossom.

God wants you to work with Him during the season after a break-up and listen as His whispers wisdom into your heart. Follow God's lead, for He has ordered the times and seasons for a reason: *'There is a time for everything, a season for every activity under heaven… A time to grieve and a time to dance… A time to search and a time to lose… A time to tear and a time to mend' (Ecclesiastes 3: 1–7).*

The good news is that no matter what season you are in, it is always the right time to draw closer to God because nothing that you or I go through can interrupt the flow of His love. He is our best friend and wants to talk to us about everything that happens in our lives. There is no need to wonder how He will respond to what you say, no matter what you're relationships have looked like. He will always be as open, gentle, and kind as He was with the Samaritan woman at the well *(John 4: 18)* and give you the grace and strength you need to feel good about your life and future again.

Reflection

Do you take the pain of a relationship break-up to the Lord or do you emotionally limp your way to the next available guy? Do you think that time alone is important to your healing? Why or why not? You are important to God and He doesn't want you to hobble from one relationship to the next! What is still hurting from a previous relationship that you can take to God in prayer this week?

Prayer

Dear Lord, I am still hurting over the break up of _____.
I feel _____ and I don't want to rush into another relationship with these feelings. Please grant me the patience to allow myself time to heal. Help me allow You the time to minister to my needs.

Broken

'You won't die!' the serpent hissed. (Genesis 3: 4)

Since the time of Adam and Eve's fall, the enemy has circulated false reports about the nature of God and His ways. Satan would have us believe that love is painful, hard to obtain, prone to fail and can never be trusted. The enemy will support his schemes by pointing to our disappointments and use them to keep us convinced of his lies.

God's true nature was displayed in the life of Christ. In Christ, we see real love demonstrated – He was patient, kind, accepting of others, hopeful, and persistent. His love overcame Satan and his kingdom of darkness. Jesus has silenced all the lies you have believed about God, yourself, and relationships. In the following devotionals, I share my brokenness and how God's power and the truth of His word healed and set me free.

You can hope again

Why am I discouraged? Why so sad? I will put my hope in God!
(Psalm 43: 5)

It was a grey, cloudy Saturday afternoon when I found them
together. After so many years of broken relationships, I thought
that I had finally found my Mr. Right. I thought he was different
from the other men I had dated and I never dreamed that one
day he would break my heart the same way the others did.

I was angry with myself for trusting again. What a fool I had
been! Would I never learn my lesson? How could I be so stupid?
Why did I keep doing this to myself? Why did he do this to me?
What did she have that I didn't? As a torrent of tears fell and
these questions raced through my mind, I was overwhelmed
by humiliation and rage. I felt my heart break and a tidal wave
of despair swept in.

I drove away from the scene with a dead feeling inside. My hope
of finding a loyal and faithful love was firmly shattered. All the
years of loss, compounded with this new betrayal, obliterated the
last glimmer of hope I had for finding happiness. From childhood
to this moment, I had accumulated a backlog of disappointment
and disillusion. This was one loss too many. I shut down, thinking
I would never again recover. I vowed to hate men for the rest of
my life. I searched for relief at the bottom of a wine glass and, for
a few short hours, tried to forget my sorrows.

The cruel reality of my past stood before me. I had tried many
times to stop the endless cycle of disappointment, but nothing
had changed. I could think of no new possible solutions, and in
despair I screamed out to God, 'I've tried everything to change
my life!' He gently replied, 'Yes, but you haven't tried me.' He
was right; I had always turned my back on Him. I felt a glimmer

of hope—perhaps following Him would change my life the way I so desperately needed. After a season of deliberation, I finally chose to listen to God. The Holy Spirit came into my heart, and I knew in that moment my life had changed. Suddenly, life seemed full of possibilities. The Lord restored my hope. I no longer fixated on the past; I looked to what God would do for me in the future. The new life I now have has surpassed all my expectations.

No matter how great the betrayal in your life or how painful your losses, what Christ did for me, He can do for you, too. God knows how to give hope to the hopeless and help those who have been crushed. *'He heals the brokenhearted, binding up their wounds' (Psalm 147: 3)*. God knows how to help you – absolutely nothing is too difficult for His healing power to overcome *(Matthew 19: 26)*. You can trust in God to restore your life because His word says His plans are not to harm you, but to give you hope and a future *(Jeremiah 29: 11)* and God never lies. Give Him a chance, like I did, and you will realise the power of His word.

Reflection

Are you broken-hearted? Have betrayals and pain taken away your hope? Do you feel cursed to keep reaping the same outcomes? When you ask God into your heart, He will give you a new life. Start by confessing your hurts and, in faith, ask Jesus to heal you of your wounds. Be open and honest about how you feel and ask Him to cleanse you of any wrong attitudes such as bitterness, hate, anger, and vengefulness. From now on, choose to follow where God says to go. He will give you a new heart and a new life of hope that will ensure your past ways of living are truly behind you.

Prayer

*Dear Jesus, I having been trying to solve my problems by myself
and things have not changed. I have been disappointed in love.
I keep making the same mistakes and I am in despair, wondering
how I can go on. Today Lord, I am choosing to listen to Your
instructions and follow You. Please help me and show me the way
out of my despair.*

Unconditional love is yours

The unfailing love of the Lord never ends! (Lamentations 3: 22)

I have loved you, my people, with an everlasting love. With unfailing love I have drawn you to myself. (Jeremiah 31: 3)

My boyfriend said he loved me, but then he gave his love to someone else. I was once the perfect girl for him, but then he started to find fault with me. One minute I was loved and adored, the next, he was walking out on me. After several similar disappointments, I started to believe that love never lasted long. In fact, I started to wait for the break-up every time I met someone new.

I came to God believing that His love would be set on conditions. I messed up, failed, and did some things I knew God would not find pleasing and I wondered when He would throw me away. I secretly feared that it was only a matter of time before He became exhausted and walked out on me, too.

After making many mistakes, I found out that His love for me was unconditional. He didn't pursue me one day and walk away the next. He has been the one Person that has stayed by my side through everything. He said He would never throw us away, *(Isaiah 41: 9)* nor forsake us *(Deuteronomy 31: 6)*, and I found His words to be true.

When you start to know for yourself that God's love is unconditional, you will stop waiting to be rejected. You'll know in your heart that love never fails, is patient, and is long-suffering. You'll know that when God loves you, He loves without limits.

God wants to give you an experience of His permanency in your life so that you rely on Him and not people for an unending and unfailing love. When you understand the nature of His eternal love, you'll stop losing hope when people let you down.

If you build your hope and security on the foundation of God's unconditional love, you will be able to believe in relationships again and adjust your expectations of finding perfect love in imperfect people. Your understanding of God and how He loves others will make a difference in your outlook on life. You will know it's possible to have a relationship that is not full of rejection and your faith will help you not give up on people so easily.

God wants you to know His love is not conditional. If you have not experienced this magnificent truth, start by getting to know God. You will discover that His love is unfailing and never-ending.

Reflection

If you believe that love does not last, you have the opportunity to change your beliefs by learning about God's love. Experiencing His unfailing love is the key to having restored hope. Decide today to give God a chance to help you learn about the true nature of His love.

Prayer

Dear Lord, I want to know what it's like to have someone stand beside me and never leave. Your love is faithful and unfailing. I put my trust in You today to help me experience and know deep in my heart that lasting love is possible.

There is healing for pain

Wine produces mockers; liquor leads to brawls. Whoever is led astray by drink cannot be wise. (Proverbs 20: 1)

We had planned to see each other that evening, but with every passing hour, I had to face the fact that he had stood me up again. Completely distraught, I went to the local shop and purchased some beer. For a few hours, I was able to numb my feelings until I finally passed out. I was fifteen years old and had found a dangerous solution for dealing with pain.

At the peak of my relationship and career problems, my drinking habit escalated out of control. One day as I sat at home drinking myself into a stupor, I started to cry. I wanted to stop drinking but I didn't know how. I ran out into the garden, as if trying to run away from the wine. I prayed to God for self-control, but I ran back into the house for another drink, feeling guilty for my inability to stop myself.

One night while I was smoking cannabis, I felt God calling me to pray. The urge would not leave until I gave in. I went to my bedroom and fell on my knees. I was too high to talk, so I just sat there in God's presence, wondering why He would want me near Him while I was in that state. The experience taught me something about God's love for me: I didn't have to clean up to be loved; I didn't have to change to be wanted. God loved me so much that He reached out to me in my worst moments.

Not long after this experience, I accepted Jesus into my life. I was so caught up in the joy of being saved that I totally forgot about drinking and smoking. The Lord removed my desire to forget about my problems and began healing my pain.

Once upon a time, when I used men to feel loved, I used drink and drugs to deal with the bad feelings inside, but neither one of them solved my problems. Now I am free, because Christ set me free. The same power that helped me is available to you. If you have reached your worst moments in life, cry out to God. He is there right beside you, ready to save and ready to heal.

Reflection

What do you use to medicate your pain? This could be anything: overspending, eating, using stimulants or drugs, sex, or gambling. Are you caught in an addictive cycle? Be honest about your addiction and work on finding the root of the problem. Seek God for healing and watch as He moves through direct intervention or the service of others to release you from the power of addiction.

Prayer

Dear God, my addictions are too powerful for me. I can't change by myself. I ask You to be my strength and my Saviour. Deliver me, O Lord, for I come to You in great need.

God himself will heal you

So why do you keep on following rules of the world, such as, 'Don't handle, don't eat, don't touch'. These rules may seem wise because they require strong devotion, humility, and severe bodily discipline. But they have no effect when it comes to conquering a person's evil thoughts and desires (Colossians 2: 20, 23).

In my mid-teens, I felt that there was something missing in my life. Around that time, I met three Christians who introduced me to God. Up until that time, my parents had left it up to me to decide what I wanted to believe.

I found I enjoyed Bible studies and after being baptised, I spent about eighteen months attending church, trying to develop a personal relationship with Christ. I thought I was building this relationship by doing everything right: I attended services, read my Bible, dressed conservatively, and never mixed with 'sinners'. I was probably one of the most religious young people that attended my church at the time!

After that initial year-and-a-half, the cracks began to appear in my faith. I found my walk with God to be a burden and the harder I tried to keep up with religious rules and expectations, the worse I felt about myself. The more I did, the more it seemed was demanded of me. No longer able to take the strain, I decided to leave the church.

The world seemed to offer me liberty while Christianity offered a lot of rules and regulations. After feeling so controlled, I longed to experience freedom, which I defined as pursuing adventure and fun and chasing what the world had to offer. I threw off my heavy coat of religion and ran out of the church as fast and far away as I could. I didn't forsake my belief in God's existence; I just couldn't serve Him the way I thought I was expected to.

For the next fifteen years, I lived my life on my terms and did whatever I thought would make me happy. My efforts failed, however, and I found myself caught in a cycle of bad behaviours that led me to continually repeat painful mistakes. There were times when I felt a deep, gnawing ache of emptiness inside of me. I tried to run from this feeling, but I could never escape. I would occasionally pick up my Bible in search of comfort, but, as I believed God was very exacting and hard to please, I felt stuck in a difficult position. Even though I was no longer satisfied with what I found in the world, doing things on my own still felt safer than serving a harsh God. I thought I had to do something to earn God's approval and love, and though, at times, I attempted to change before I came to Him, my sins were too strong for me to overcome them.

It took a complete breakdown at the age of thirty-two for me to finally admit I couldn't live on my own anymore. The Holy Spirit had been moving in my heart and had shown me glimpses of God's kindness. In sheer desperation, I reached out, begging God to show me another way to live—and He did. He poured out His love and acceptance and He delivered me from myself. Finally, I found the freedom I had craved all those years ago. I realised that the love I sought from men was poured out on me in Christ; He was the one I had been searching for in each relationship. I fell in love with Him and when I looked back at my life, I saw that He had never left my side.

Religion does not offer fulfilment for our deep longings to be loved; instead of freedom, religion only offers another way to be controlled. If rules and regulations could save, we would not need Jesus. We need a personal encounter with God that leads to a personal relationship with Him. This relationship is the only thing that can release us from our desperate attempts to find love in illegitimate ways. Connect with Jesus and He will set you free! God is at peace with you. Run to Him and let your life overflow with the love you have always been searching for!

Reflection

Is your walk with God focused more on performance or relationship? Do you feel judged and condemned when you make mistakes or do you walk secure in God's love despite the mistakes you sometimes make? Open your heart to God and give Him your pain. Ask Him to confirm His love for you so that you might be assured of His acceptance.

Prayer

Lord, I thought You were a harsh and judgemental God. I ran away thinking You demanded change before I could come to You. Thank You Jesus, for saving my life and reassuring me that I can come to You just as I am because I am deeply loved and wanted. I accept the gift of new life that You offer me.

Find yourself again

Keep me from lying to myself. (Psalm 119: 29)

I didn't need to tell long contorted stories to lie. I simply didn't speak my mind, pretended to agree, and did whatever was necessary to maintain peace in my relationships, despite going against my conscience. All those years of pretending and lying, however, eventually caught up with me; I suddenly realised one day that I had lost all sense of who I was.

Though I wanted to blame past boyfriends, I knew it was my faulty beliefs that had led me to where I was. I had spent so long believing that I had to compromise and change in order to keep a guy that I had become a clone of each man I dated.

The Lord showed me that He lives in truth and honesty. He doesn't pretend to be somebody He is not and He doesn't want us to pretend, either. Sometimes we find it difficult to be ourselves, especially when we have been criticised and rejected by others. The ramifications of hiding our true selves, however, are far more daunting than any potential disapproval we may face; our dishonesty can lead us on the wrong path in life *(Proverbs 11: 5)*.

The only way I could stop disappearing was to be honest with myself. I needed to admit how I really felt, what I really thought, and what I really wanted. This kind of personal integrity helps us in our relationships, for we learn not to hide who we are or pretend that things are fine when we know they are not! We also give a man a chance to fall in love with us based on reality when we are comfortable being ourselves in front of him.

Opposite is a selection of godly principles that will help you discover the real you—the person God has created you to be:

Acknowledge your needs and desires *(Mark 10: 51–52)*. God is interested in everything you have to say and wants to hear from you. Admit what is on your heart and share your needs with Jesus. His gentleness makes it easy to speak up.

Be honest with others and say how you feel. Let them know when you don't like the way they are treating you and encourage behaviours that you do appreciate. You will never receive what you need from others if you do not speak truthfully.

Trust God to be your Protector *(Psalm 121: 5)*. This will help you overcome your fear of speaking the truth. Pretending can lead you to make wrong decisions and cause you to lose yourself again.

Believe that you are a significant member of God's family *(1 Corinthians 12: 27)*. Challenge any voice that tells you your thoughts and feelings are not important. Learn to be yourself with others.

God's way of thinking produces life and power. Learn to expose your own limiting beliefs so that you can adopt God's mindset in all that you do *(Philippians 2: 5)*.

Allow God to guide you *(Isaiah 58: 11)*. Trust that He won't lead you astray and listen to His counsel. Don't harm yourself by trying to do things your own way. Notice the way God does things, then fall into line *(Ecclesiastes 7: 13)*. Trust that His way is the best.

Believe that God rewards your faith. If something goes against your conscience, understand that doing it will be wrong for you *(Romans 14: 23)*. Learn to do everything in faith, with a clear conscience.

Reflection

Maintaining your identity means being honest with God, yourself and others. What have you been afraid to admit or express to others? Have your insecurities caused you to lose a part of yourself? Which principle listed above can you integrate into your life today? (Note: Unsafe people may use your vulnerability against you, so share the deepest parts of yourself with those who are healthy and can keep a confidence.)

Prayer

Dear God, telling the truth has made me feel like a willing victim to pain. I now see that suppressing my thoughts and opinions keeps all the hurt and pain locked up inside of me. I want to live in freedom and truth. Lord, I come to You in confession, asking for change. From this moment forward, I want to find out who You created me to be.

Live!

*No one cared a fig for you. No one did one thing to care for you
tenderly in these ways. You were thrown out into a vacant lot and
left there, dirty and unwashed—a newborn nobody wanted. And
then I came by. I saw you all miserable and bloody. Yes, I said to you,
lying there helpless and filthy, 'Live!' (Ezekiel 16: 5, 6 MSG).*

It seemed that I was never free from hating myself; I felt like I had
a sign on my forehead that said, "I am a loser". I sensed that there
was something very wrong with me, but I could never quite
figure out the exact nature of my inadequacy.

When a young man from my neighbourhood raped me
because I would not date him, I saw the experience as further
proof that I was a terrible person. I buried my feelings of
shame, put on a brave face, and tried to not think about what
happened. Yet inside I was barren. I played it safe, withdrew
into myself, and never attempted to make a go of the dream
I had for my future.

I thought that after a period of time, I would get over what had
happened. However, the memories would overwhelm me and
I would cry myself to sleep. It wasn't until eighteen years later, in
the safety of a counsellor's presence, that I was able to go back
to that night and face what happened.

God gave me the strength to talk about my self-hatred, as well
as the rape itself, and how it had further damaged my self-
image. Jesus showed me that, by bringing my wounds into
the light, I would be healed and restored. He assured me that
the way I had been treated by others could not take away my
dignity or the value He had placed on me. Thereafter, as I found
healing, I became emotionally and mentally stronger. In God's
strength, I made the decision that I would not allow my life to

be destroyed by other people's destructive behaviours or the lies I had once accepted about myself.

No one has the right to ignore our refusals and abuse our bodies, minds, or hearts, whether once or over a period of time. The wounds that are caused by abuse are very real and require healing. They can damage our identity and self-worth if we do not face how we have been hurt. Do not ignore your pain, hoping it will go away. The Lord does not take sides with those who commit evil, so don't believe that He is indifferent to or passive about what has happened to you. God always sides with the oppressed; He will *'bring justice to the orphans and the oppressed, so people can no longer terrify them' (Psalm 10: 18)*.

God does not want you to remain a victim or be hindered from taking the path that will give you back your life. You have a future that is better than anything you dare to believe is possible because God is your Redeemer and Restorer. God will give you back more than you have lost and He will take away all pain and shame from your life.

God's healing over my rape experience has been so complete that, though the memories remain, the darkness and pain have gone. I have risen from the ashes of abuse and reclaimed God's purpose for me—a purpose the devil tried to steal. There is hope and there is life beyond the grave of rape!

Don't give up! Take your broken heart to Christ and let Him set you free! In my case, the Lord used a Christian counsellor and time alone with Him to heal my heart. Trust Him to minister to you in the way you need Him to, and don't resist reaching out for help. Don't allow another person's wrong actions to define your identity and rob you of life. God wants to fill you with hope so you can offer His salvation to those who are suffering and in need of your testimony. Heed God's call to live!

Reflection

Working through pain and allowing the Lord to heal you is paramount. You need to firmly agree with God that your value is not dictated by how others have treated you. It is also important to progress toward forgiveness, as hatred and bitterness will keep you locked in the past and rob you of what God is doing in your life today. Remember, God's command to you today is 'Live!'

Prayer

O God, I am hurting so much; the pain is deep within my heart and I am so angry and ashamed. I hate myself and I hate the person who has hurt me. God, please save me. Heal me. I give my pain and shame to You. I release the person who has hurt me into Your hands. Lead me to forgiveness so that I can be free from the past. I want to live!

You are forgiven

Once again you will have compassion on us. You will trample our sins under your feet and throw them into the depths of the ocean! (Micah 7: 19)

I had suffered bouts of depression over the years, but I was surprised to discover that some of those dark days were directly linked to drastic actions I had taken in the past.

As I prayed and listened to the Lord speak, He led me to think about my decisions to have abortions. Years ago, I had chosen this route as a means of dealing with unwanted situations I had gotten myself into. I envisioned Christ standing before me with a look of sadness and pain in His eyes. I was a little ashamed because I felt numb and could not identify with His grief. I had not wanted to remember what had happened and had pushed those memories away. Jesus chose to remind me about this part of my past so I could be healed.

I didn't even know that I needed healing. I had taken a risk with men that were not interested in a relationship. When I fell pregnant, I was deeply afraid and confused. I didn't want to pay the price for my indiscretions. I didn't think I could cope and argued within myself that I was too young, already had children, or had no money to take care of another baby. I knew the father wasn't going to stick around and I was not willing to face life raising more children alone. I believed that I had good reasons not to go through with the pregnancies.

The Lord peers into the hearts of His children and sees all the things that lay therein that we don't see *(Hebrews 4: 12–13)*. Inside I was hurting, but I had buried my feelings so deeply that I couldn't see what was causing my pain. As I began to remember my actions, I felt a great sense of loss and, for the first time in my life, I was able to cry and mourn. Waves of guilt, remorse, and grief enveloped my soul, while the Lord comforted me with the reassurance that He wanted to relieve me of the wounds my actions had caused. As I broke down and cried, I saw the Lord crying with me and I knew in that moment I was not grieving alone. More importantly, I knew I had Christ's forgiveness. Today, I do not suffer from depression.

If you have been through an abortion, I understand how painful the experience is. Women are not informed about the emotional consequences that abortion causes. Thankfully, we have a God that is able to remove our pain and wash away our sins, casting them into the depths of the sea, forgiven and forgotten. God can heal and remove all depression, guilt, sadness, grief, and spiritual darkness associated with abortion. Do not shrink away in shame or hide what is causing you pain. He is waiting for you to come. Reach out and be healed.

Reflection

Abortion is not God's will, but remember that with God there is hope and restoration for us. David leaned on this hope after the death of his child saying, 'I will go to him one day, but he cannot return to me' (2 Samuel 12: 23). Today, God offers you forgiveness and a new start with Him. Choose to accept this offer, forgive yourself, and continue your journey, pressing toward the plans God has in store for you.

Prayer

Dear Jesus, I've carried this pain and guilt, wondering how I could ever be forgiven. I think about my unborn child; I grieve my loss and place it in your hands. Lord, thank You for forgiving me and giving me hope for the future.

The truth will set you free

If we say we have no sin, we are only fooling ourselves and refusing to accept the truth. If we claim we have not sinned, we are calling God a liar and showing that his word has no place in our hearts. (1 John 1: 8, 10)

I was consumed with one question: how could he feel no remorse for the way he was treating me? He flirted with other women in front of me, called me names, and found pleasure in putting me down in front of others. He had a subtle way of criticising my achievements, looks, opinions, and decisions and twisted things so everything became my fault.

His lack of guilt hurt deeply but he would laugh off my protestations, saying he didn't think he was doing anything wrong. He claimed that I was in a mess and even suggested that I needed to see a psychologist.

The longer I stayed with him the more I believed him. Perhaps it was me and as I wanted things to be good between us, I tried harder to please. When I turned to others for help, I could never find an answer that gave me any sense of peace. Their advice was to leave him, but that had done nothing to empower me because I was too consumed with guilt. I couldn't see that I was in a relationship with a man that felt I was to blame for his behaviour. Nor could I see that I was a woman who thought his issues were somehow her fault.

Being disrespected ruined my confidence and sense of self-worth and took away my ability to resist further abuse. It was a dark place to be. I felt constantly condemned and worthless and it was only through the light of God's words that I started to understand just how battered my mind had become.

It has taken a long time to undo the damage, but now I stand free from condemnation and can recognise the abuse mentality. I no longer take the blame for everyone's mistakes and can confront issues that are hurtful to me rather than discounting my feelings.

If this situation sounds familiar to you, be at peace. You are not to blame for anyone's critical and abusive behaviours. One of the hallmarks of healthy relationships is being able to take ownership of our actions and confessing when we are wrong *(James 5: 16),* but abusive people are unwilling to do this. However, just because they resist the truth, that doesn't make their opinions correct. Pour your heart and your mind into God and His word and allow His truth to become the basis for your beliefs and opinions. His truth will set you free.

Let Jesus know that you will no longer believe the put-downs and ask Him to remove your false guilt. Claim this promise: *'Come to me, all of you who are weary and carry heavy burdens, and I will give you rest. Take my yoke upon you. Let me teach you, because I am humble and gentle, and you will find rest for your souls. For my yoke fits perfectly, and the burden I give you is light'* (Matthew 11: 28–29).

You are not alone. God sees the darkness and misery you are in and waits for you to turn to Him so He can set you free.

Reflection

Are you shouldering unnecessary blame? What have you taken responsibility for that does not belong to you? Find out how emotional abuse works. Make God's truth the final authority in your life so that you can dismiss destructive criticism and insults without condemnation.

Prayer

Dear Lord, You gave Your Son to me that I might live free from condemnation and guilt. I have allowed the words of others to control me to the point that I have lost all sense of worth and dignity. Jesus, please take this burden from my neck. From now on, I choose to listen to the truth and work out my problems according to Your word. Help me make Your words the final authority in my life.

You are precious

I am a worm and not a man. I am scorned and despised by all!
(Psalm 22: 6)

When you look in the mirror, what thoughts cross your mind?
Do you like yourself or do you hate what you see? Do you value
yourself as a child of God or do you feel unloved by Him?

For many years, I hated myself. I was never popular or outgoing
and somehow I felt that meant something was wrong with
me. I forced myself to go to parties and clubs in an effort to fit
in, when my real desire was to stay at home and read or hang
out with a small group of friends. I thought I was boring and
rejected myself so much that I even had a hard time listening to
people say my name.

The relationship I had with myself didn't only affect my peace
of mind. My poor self-image prevented me from experiencing
peace and harmony with those closest to me. As my mind
was conditioned to find fault with myself, it was impossible to
switch to thinking good and uplifting thoughts about others.
I found it hard to accept my loved ones and focused on what
they did wrong rather than what they did right. When I dated,
I worried about allowing men to get to know me, afraid they
would discover the monsters I saw in myself.

As I spent time in prayer and read God's word, something
started to happen. I was directed to many scriptures about God's
love and they started to appeal to me. I began to trust God
with my inner world, sharing my secret thoughts. As He gently
responded, reassuring me of His love, the critical inner voice I had
lived with all my life started to lose its power over my mind.

Receiving God's love helped me begin to respond differently to
my loved ones. The word says that when we receive God's love

we are able to love others *(1 John 4: 19)*. Instead of isolating myself, I took risks in forming friendships. I learnt how to encourage others and help them turn to the God of comfort, too.

The Lord does not want you to reject what He has accepted. Train yourself to agree with His word and see what He sees. God offers these promises to you:

Though you feel horrible, the Lord sees you as His beautiful possession, a royal diadem in His hands (Isaiah 62: 3).

Though you think you are bad, the Lord sees you, His creation, as good (Genesis 1: 31).

Though you feel forsaken, the Lord gathered you to Himself (Isaiah 62: 4).

Though you feel rejected, the Lord has cared for you as His child (Ezekiel 16: 1–8).

Though you were like a young bride rejected by her man, the Lord says He will be like a husband to you (Isaiah 54: 4-6).

Reflection

Meditate on Psalm 139. God says that you are His marvellous creation, planned and accepted. Reflect on these things and let God's truth heal your self-rejection. Personalise these scriptures to remind yourself that God sees you the way He sees His Son: loved, accepted, and very precious in His sight.

Prayer

Dear God, I have felt so unloved! I have hated myself so much that I can no longer find anything good in myself or in my life! Lord, reveal Your love to me. Comfort me. I want to know what it is like to experience love and acceptance. I ask You to come into my heart right now. Thank You Lord, for Your comfort and for answering my prayer.

You are accepted

Don't look down on me, you fair city girls. (Song of Songs 1: 6)

As a child, I listened to insensitive comments made about certain parts of my body. When I became a teenager, those 'problem areas' became an obsession, and I constantly worried about what others thought of me.

In my twenties, I became an aerobics teacher. As so many women around me suffered from complexes about their appearance, I had more opportunities to fixate on my own body and compare myself to others. In my mind, I linked my appearance to my acceptance, and I was very sensitive to what a guy thought about my looks. To ensure I was attractive, I followed a strict diet and sometimes worked out twice a day, a routine that did not include the classes I taught. Reshaping my body did not yield the results I expected, as it didn't change the way I felt inside, nor reward me with the love I desired. No matter how many compliments I received, the praise was never enough. I hated the way I looked and wore baggy clothes to hide my imperfections.

As the years passed, I added other anxieties. Battling for a great body was now overshadowed by the reality of getting older. Suddenly I wasn't just fighting flab; I was engaged in a battle against wrinkles and losing my youth! I knew I wasn't living in freedom, but I didn't know how to change my feelings of inadequacy.

In another episode of panic and fear, I sought the Lord for help. This time a scripture came to mind: *'I will be your God throughout your lifetime—until your hair is white with age. I made you, and I will care for you. I will carry you along and save you' (Isaiah 46: 4).* Then I heard the Lord whisper the word 'loved'. I knew in that moment that He had loved me when I was born and that he would love me when I was old and grey. I felt Him assure my heart that I was loved no matter how old I was and that I was precious in His sight.

Finally, I could see! I had been battling all these years, not to obtain the perfect body, but to know deep in the recesses of my heart if I was truly accepted. God answered my heart's question with a resounding yes! I had only seen the way the world accepted people. God wanted to show me that real love would never accept me one day, then cast me aside the next because I no longer fit some unattainable standard of beauty. God assured me that He loved all of me and that He would never change His mind just because my body was changing.

God wants to help every woman who struggles with a poor body image. As you move closer to God, His love will minister to the real issues beneath your anxieties. Know that you are loved just as you are and rejoice in and appreciate your body. Shout out with David: *'Thank you for making me so wonderfully complex! Your workmanship is marvellous' (Psalm 139: 14)*. As you praise God for His workmanship, remember that He also promised to make all things new, including your body! One day we will have the ultimate body, free from disease and the defects of sin: *'The corpse that's planted is no beauty, but when it's raised, it's glorious. Put in the ground weak, it comes up powerful' (I Corinthians 15: 43 MSG)*. Now isn't that a body worth waiting for?

Reflection

Jesus was never critical of anyone's physical appearance (Mark 1: 40–42). Does your self-image need the loving touch of Christ? Do you place more value on looks or character? Read 1 Samuel 16: 7. How did Samuel go about finding the right man for the job? What did God teach him to do? Do you need to change your focus from appearances to

matters of the heart in order to be healed? Another way
of overcoming a poor body image or fear of ageing is to
develop deeper and more meaningful friendships. That way
you will not feel you have to rely on your looks or youth to
feel accepted and loved.

Prayer

*Dear Lord, I've watched Hollywood women be rejected for
aging. I've been the recipient of unkind comments about my
looks and I have found fault with myself. Yet Lord, I am Your
marvellous masterpiece! Heal me of my poor self-image. Give me
joy where there is now fear. May my lips only ever speak of Your
workmanship and recount Your faithful promise that I will receive
a new body when You return!*

Let go

The Lord says 'I will give you back what you lost'. (Joel 2: 25)

God once allowed me to imagine a kind of picture of a man who lived in a dry and barren land. This man was seated beside a well, using a broken piece of pottery to scrape the dregs of water from his bucket. A woman sat opposite him, staring intensely at the water, hoping he would give her a drink, too. The man was very guarded over his water supply, yet the woman continued to stare, craving the water. Every so often he would offer her a sip, but it didn't quench the woman's thirst.

As I prayed about this image, God allowed me to see that the man sitting at the well represented people in our families and that the water represented the love we hoped would be shown to us. The scene I had imagined made me realise that, during my upbringing, my need of love and acceptance had not been fully met because those around me had not enough 'water' for themselves. As I thought about this truth, I felt a shift in my expectations. I realised that, like me, my family was broken and in need of Christ's love. I heard God tell me that it was time to let go of the expectations I had placed on my family. It wasn't easy, but as I let go of my demands, I learnt to accept where they were and work towards being at peace.

Letting go made me realise that I had built a similar hope around others. I latched on to people who had little to give and spent my time arguing and fighting over things they couldn't offer me. As I no longer felt the need to do this, I found it easier to accept people instead of continually finding fault in them. I have learned to develop different levels of friendship and intimacy in my relationships, instead of using an intense all-or-nothing approach.

The Lord wants us to learn about love from our families, but, because of sin, we each carry our imperfections and weaknesses into our parenting. We have all experienced various levels of pain, disappointment, or loss in our families, which has marred how we see ourselves and how we go about forging relationships with others. We can choose to stay broken, angry, and unforgiving, or we can accept that we are all damaged and thirsty as a result of negative influences in our lives, such as imperfect parenting or abuse.

Unfortunately, we don't always recognise that God can restore the brokenness caused by the pain of our childhoods. Listen to His word: *'Don't be afraid, because you won't be put to shame. Don't be discouraged, because you won't be disgraced. You'll forget the shame you've had since you were young' (Isaiah 54: 4 GWT).* His plan is to give us a new start: *'For you have been born again. Your new life did not come from your earthly parents because the life they gave you will end in death. But this new life will last forever because it comes from the eternal, living word of God' (1 Peter 1: 23).*

Isn't that great news? He has purposed that no matter what we have inherited or been through with our parents, we can receive a new life in Him—a life that will not repeat the cycle or be taken away from us!

Consider this carefully: The Lord does not intend to leave you in a state of brokenness caused by your upbringing. He offers you a new start and a new life. You can decide to let God heal the inner wounds from your childhood or you can remain angry, hurt, and bitter. If you choose His healing, He will free you from the crippling power of your past and restore to you the years that were stripped away by disappointment and pain.

Reflection

Are you still striving to gain attention and affection from your parents or others? Do you feel angry and hurt because you missed out on knowing what it's like to come from a

'normal' family? Give your pain and anger to the Lord. Tell Him how you feel and release your disappointments to Him. The Lord will restore everything you have lost. Be patient as He heals your heart and moves you beyond this place.

Prayer

Lord, it hurts to let go and face the fact that I can't have the type of relationship I wanted with _____. I know You want me to move on from this place, so that I am no longer stuck in the past, trying to fix things I can never repair. I want to start the process of letting go and walking forward with You.

You can find safe people

There are 'friends' who destroy each other, but a real friend sticks closer than a brother. (Proverbs 18: 24)

It is such a blessing to be able to turn to a friend for help and know that we are being listened to and loved. I have a couple of very close friends who offer their support, pray over me, and give honest feedback. I know I can trust them with what I share. I can leave their company, confident that I will not become the subject of gossip. Without my friends, I don't know how I would have made it through some very difficult times. I know that Jesus brought these people into my life and I am thankful, because I remember a time when I didn't have this kind of friendship in my life.

Some of my relationships suffered because of the influence of a friend. I didn't see her mistrust of men as anything to worry about; after all, I agreed with her that men were no good. Because she was my friend, I trusted her wisdom and insight. I leaned on her advice, even though it was heavily loaded with fear, judgement, and suspicion. When I was at my lowest and turned to her for encouragement, her advice was far from uplifting. Her words left me more depressed, less hopeful, and greatly confused.

If our friends are hurt, bitter, and angry about the same issues we face, they cannot be the type of people to speak life and wisdom into our lives. Their views won't be balanced. If they have a bad attitude towards men, they will only blame our dates when we experience problems and will not help us learn how to deal with conflicts in the long run. If they are jealous of a relationship, their envy will poison their ability to give the right support.

The influence of friends in our healing process cannot be underestimated. We need to avoid those whose advice keeps us stuck where we are. We cannot have freedom and success if we heed those who are quick to blame and fault find. We need to surround ourselves with people who are successful in the areas we struggle with and learn from them. We can seek out uplifting individuals who will hold us accountable and encourage our continual development. If this kind of friendship is not immediately available, seek professional help from mentors, counsellors, or teachers for balanced advice.

Of course, your greatest friend and cheerleader will always be Jesus. When our hearts are comforted by His presence, we learn how to love and become more discerning of those who love Him, too.

May God grant you the blessing of true friendship, so that you can continue to grow in Christ. May you and your friends be a people who have 'the tongue of the learned' that *'know how to speak a word in season to him who is weary' (Isaiah 50: 4 NKJV).*

Reflection

What type of people are your friends and what type of friend are you? Are you growing and becoming more Christ-like as a result of your friendships or you being led astray? In what ways might you start to find and build safe friendships outside of your dating life so that you have people to turn to?

Prayer

Dear Lord, the people I have chosen to hang out with have not always had the best influence on me. Help me seek out people who care about my welfare. I thank You for _____, with whom I share the gift of friendship. Thank You for their love and support.

A new start

You will show me the way of life. (Psalm 16: 11)

I like to think that God caused Adam to sleep
while He created Eve so that He would be the first
person she gazed upon when she opened her eyes.
By giving Eve time alone with her Creator, God
ensured that she knew to whom she belonged and
in whose image she was made. Her identity secure,
Eve was then able to take her position as helper to
Adam and co-ruler over the earth.

Each of us needs time alone with God and with
safe members of His family so that we grow
accustomed to being loved. These relationships are
healing and help us learn about healthy and abuse-
free interactions.

In the following stories, I share what my healthy
relationships have taught me, how they helped me
grow, and how they shaped my understanding of
waiting on God's timing when I started accepting
dates again. I hope that you will be encouraged by
them and that you will let God take as much time
as He needs to restore you. Be patient as He works
on healing and transforming you into a whole
woman in Christ.

Start where you are!

I can do everything with the help of Christ who gives me the strength I need. (Philippians 4: 13)

Unable to work with a bullying boss, I decided to leave my job, but I was worried I might not be able to find something more fulfilling. I was bored with the jobs I held in the past and I was also concerned that I did not have enough transferable skills to command the type of money I needed to stay on top of my debts. I felt trapped by my circumstances. Finally, in my desperation, I prayed for God's help. I asked that He would close the door on all the jobs that were not right for me and guide me to the best one.

As I continued applying for jobs, the strangest things started to happen! Sometimes prospective employers never received my application in the post. In one instance, a year after posting an application, I received a humorous letter from the employer stating it had only just turned up in the mail! Other times, offers of employment were strangely withdrawn with no clear reason why.

While I searched for work, my circumstances went from bad to worse. The bullying escalated, my financial debts continued to increase, and my relationship with my partner disintegrated into continual fights and arguments. I started to drink very heavily and sank into a depression. Eventually, I was signed off work while the Human Resources department investigated my complaints.

During my time off, I noticed an advertisement for a Personal Advisor to work with long-term unemployed people. I had never done this type of work before, but I felt led to apply for the job. I was asked to come in for an interview and, though I was suffering from stress and feeling extremely insecure, I made it through the appointment and left the results with God.

A few evenings later, after much internal struggle, I broke up with my boyfriend and surrendered my life to Christ. I was instantly delivered from the power of alcohol and smoking and my heaviness gave way to peace and joy. The very next morning, while enjoying the peace of God's presence, I was further overwhelmed by God's goodness when an offer of employment for the Personal Advisor position arrived through the post!

I took the job even though I felt deeply insecure and was terrified of failing. I was a new Christian, but I kept hearing God's word say, 'I can do all things through Christ who strengthens me'. Every time I felt afraid, I would repeat those words. By the end of my first year as a Personal Advisor, I was recognised for consistently reaching my targets. The even greater blessing, however, was that God had placed me in a job that would develop my skills and introduce me to people who would help prepare me for the work He has called me into now.

When I prayed to the Lord about my job, I had not yet surrendered my life completely to Him. My life was a mess and I could see no way out or way to cope without my partner. Looking back, I see that the Holy Spirit was moving and helping me to act on the bits of light that I was being shown. God met me where I was and made a way for me. He didn't wait for me to figure it all out first. He simply asked for a chance to be part of my life and made the changes for me.

It doesn't matter if you have been brought down by abusive people or other evil circumstances. Jesus made a way out for you when He overcame the power of sin on the cross. He has already sorted out your problems and knows what has to be done to get you through them. Choose to believe what He says He will do for you!

Do not entertain the idea that it's too late. Through Christ, you have power, a purpose, and an awesome work to do, complete with the gifts and talents necessary to accomplish the task. Put your trust in God and start living the life He has promised, unshaken by doubt. He died and yet He lives; He has the power to restore life to everything that is dead within you! It doesn't matter where you start or how weak you feel. Remember that you can do all things through Christ who strengthens you!

Reflection

Going it alone after a break-up can be a vulnerable and stressful time; the cost of making a new start may seem too much. Are you overwhelmed by your circumstances and can't see a way out? Do you need to bring the Lord into your problems rather than allow fear to keep you trapped? How might Philippians 4: 13 apply to your situation and help you handle your difficulties?

Prayer

Dear Lord, You are my Protector and I am Your special possession. You love me too much to leave me alone to struggle! Help me never forget that when things get so tough that I can't see a way out, You are my light in darkness. Comfort me with the knowledge that You are in the midst of my troubles, fighting for me!

Learn to rely on God

Do not be afraid, for I have ransomed you. I have called you by name; you are mine. When you go through deep waters and great trouble, I will be with you. When you go through rivers of difficulty, you will not drown! When you walk through the fire of oppression, you will not be burned up; the flames will not consume you. For I am the Lord, your God, the Holy One of Israel, your Saviour. (Isaiah 43: 1–3)

I remember the moment so clearly; I was cleaning my kitchen and worrying about how I was going to live within my income now that I was single and following God. I had been financially dependent on my partner and I began to fear that I wasn't going to survive! I couldn't see a way to manage all the debt I had accumulated. My expenses were literally three times the amount of my income. The future looked bleak when I considered my choices: I could provide food for my family instead of making house payments or we could keep our home and go hungry. As I looked at the front door, I imagined the horrible image of my children and I standing outside, suitcases in hand, while the house was being repossessed.

In fear, I began to think about going back to my ex, as he still wanted reconciliation. However, it wasn't long before I sensed the Holy Spirit asking me to combat my problems with faith. I had an opportunity to face my fear and venture into the unknown, trusting that God would take care of me. I didn't know how I was going to make it or where the money would come from, but I knew that following God was more important than securing my financial stability. I knew I would rather be homeless and free than keep my home and go back to a life of pain.

The Lord reassured me that, with His help, I would get through this difficult time. He promised me that I was not alone and that He would provide. With renewed faith, I looked away from the front door and carried on cleaning the kitchen. Having set my fears aside, I felt a peaceful assurance that I had made the right decision.

The next few years did not pass without difficulty. Each day was a test, as money shortages stretched my faith and taught me to rely on God's provision. I would start most days with no money, let alone funds for the entire month. In his faithfulness, God performed miracles, sending provision from the most unexpected sources. At times I grew tired and desperately wanted a quick way out of my financially unstable circumstances. God took me down this route, however, because He was more concerned with my training than my present comfort. I learnt a lot about my attitude towards money and my desire for instant gratification. I needed to learn to say no to impulsive buying and be aware of my cash flow.

God taught me wise money skills while I lived on an insufficient budget. At the same time, He ensured that my family did not go hungry and my bills were paid. Four years later, I achieved freedom from debt and willingly gave up my home to follow the next phase of God's plan for my life. As I continue to walk with Him, he continues to ask me to take larger steps of faith.

Don't allow money or some other material concern drive you back into a relationship that you know is causing you or your children harm. God has given you a measure of faith, so use it by trusting in His unfailing love. He is your Protector; He has already planned for your provision and made a way for you. You might not be able to see His plan at the moment, but your lack of understanding shouldn't serve as an indication that God is not meeting your needs. As you learn to wait on God, you will find that He rarely makes next week's provisions available today. He wants us to assimilate His word so we will know that He gives us what we need on a day-to-day basis. Rest in His love, for you will be safe, you will be taken care of, and all your needs will be met.

Reflection

Are financial concerns influencing your decision to stay in a relationship that you know is outside of what God wants for you? The Lord is fully aware of your needs even before you ask Him. Look to Him as the source of all your provision. When you depend on God to meet your daily needs, you will not be tempted to throw your faith aside and take matters into your own hands.

What practical steps can you take today to sort out your finances? The Lord works through many agencies and individuals to provide the right guidance. Be brave and ask for help and support.

Prayer

Dear Lord, I admit I am afraid. I fear what making a new start will mean for me financially. I am not sure I can do it. I feel so weak! Thank You God for being my strength! Today, I make You my financial provider and trust You to take care of me.

Avoid looking back

'Run for your lives!' The angels warned. 'Do not stop anywhere in the valley. And don't look back! Escape to the mountains, or you will die.' But Lot's wife looked back. (Genesis 19: 17, 26)

When we take our first steps toward a new way of living, we will almost certainly experience a season during which our commitment is tested. For example, a person who decides to get out of debt might suddenly have to exercise faith as their car breaks down, the roof springs a leak, and the dog gets sick. Our relationships are not immune from this time of testing.

I remember meeting a guy with whom I felt immediate chemistry. The attraction was very strong, as he was exactly the type of man I would have dated in the past. He kept asking for a date and, despite knowing in my heart that involving myself with him would be walking on dangerous ground, I still struggled with my desire. I started playing mind games and questioned my resolve. What if I went on one date? What if I simply called him? What if I just went for lunch with him and took along some friends? Surely that wouldn't hurt! The internal struggle was intense and the more I reasoned with myself, the more my excuses seemed plausible.

Nostalgic memories presented themselves as desirable alternatives to sticking with the new way I was living. Suddenly, old habits I willingly gave up when I was hurting didn't seem so bad after all. I was slipping back into denial and lying to myself that I wouldn't get hurt. Thankfully, God's Holy Spirit was protecting me from myself!

The first thing God told me to do was to quit struggling with my desires on my own! As I released my burden to Jesus, I felt a weight lift off my shoulders and a new understanding of my situation flooded my mind. Deep in my heart, I knew I wanted a different life. I wanted to be with a man who possessed spiritual values and was committed to being his best. Though no man in my life fit that description, I knew that didn't mean I would never meet one. I simply had to learn to wait and let go of what I knew was not good for me.

Releasing old habits to God can be painful, and it's normal to feel a sense of loss when you say no to your old desires. Be prepared to feel a bit of grief when you let go. We are taught in the word that our old desires fight with the new desires that the Holy Spirit puts in our hearts, but if we choose to follow His promptings, we will remain free *(Galatians 5: 17)*. If you don't understand this process, you might run straight back to what only feels right, fearing the new way is too difficult to embrace.

God is your Helper. He doesn't expect you to struggle with your desires on your own. You are weak and His is strong; let His power perfectly compensate for your weaknesses *(2 Corinthians 12: 9)*. Focus on what you really want in a relationship and keep your thoughts from romanticising men from your past that were not good for you. Face your future with hope saying *'I am still not all I should be, but I am focusing all my energies on this one thing: Forgetting the past and looking forward to what lies ahead, I strain to reach the end of the race and receive the prize for which God, through Christ Jesus, is calling us up to heaven' (Philippians 3: 13–14).*

Reflection

In what situations do you find yourself struggling with your old desires? Deeper growing love for God empowers you to live for Him. What scriptures can you meditate on to deepen your love? What truths can you recall when faced with temptation? What else would help you to pause and turn to God before acting? If you have done things you regret, do not despair. God came to help the weak and promises you forgiveness, restoration, and power to overcome.

Prayer

Dear Lord, You know me completely; You know where I struggle with temptation. I have entertained the idea of relationships that I know are not right for me. Search my heart, O Lord, and show me Your will, for I desire to live for You and receive Your very best for me.

Know your worth

When I look at the night sky and see the work of your fingers – the moon and the stars you have set in place – what are mortals that you should think of us, mere humans that you should care for us? (Psalm 8: 3–4)

Fifteen months after my relationship ended, I still felt the financial effects of our break-up. As Christmas arrived, I found I had no money to cover the festive season and I resigned myself to the fact I could not give my children gifts that year.

One day, a couple from my church felt led to provide some financial assistance – and the presents didn't stop there. Others also felt impressed to give, so much so that I ran out of cupboard space to store everything! My family and I love chocolate, and I couldn't help but notice God's sense of humour and thoughtfulness when He provided enough to hide the surface of our dinning room table! The fact that the Lord would prompt others to make our Christmas special made me realise how precious my family is to Him.

The need to feel significant and important is wired into each of us. God's intent is to fulfil these needs Himself as he looks after and cares for us. He wants us to know we are His children and that He takes responsibility for our care. He wants us to fully understand that all the details of our lives matter to Him. Without this understanding, we will attempt to measure our significance in other ways.

Some of us rely on our status in life or the type of jobs that we hold to determine our worth. Others focus on the amount of wealth they can produce or material things they can acquire. I thought I gained importance by being in a relationship. Having a man around, regardless of how unhealthy the match, made me feel wanted. Since I thought I only had significance when someone loved me, I quickly lost all sense of self-worth when a relationship ended. I had nothing outside of the relationship letting me know I was still of value. Without a man, I felt lost and alone. I would accuse myself of being a loser and believed that men couldn't wait to get away from me.

Though you may have sunk into a cesspool of negativity about your personal value, a long time ago, before you were even born, the Lord determined your worth. He magnificently displayed how precious you are to Him by sacrificing the life of His Son. Base your significance on the God you belong to and the price He paid to purchase your life and there will be no need to prove your worth in other ways. In Christ, we have the security of knowing that, regardless of the people and possessions around us, we are still of priceless value. Work on seeing yourself in the way He sees you. Without this foundation, you will never firmly determine your worth and will continue to look to a man or material things to make that determination for you.

Be grounded in the truth by meditating on these promises because God wrote them just for you!

God knows you down to the tiniest detail; he knows the number of hairs on your head *(Matthew 10: 30)*.

He sings songs of rejoicing over you *(Zephaniah 3: 17)*.

He has engraved your name on the palm of his hand *(Isaiah 49: 16)*.

He declares His eternal faithfulness to you *(Psalm 100: 5)*.

He says that you are precious and that He loves you *(Isaiah 43: 4)*.

He loved you enough to die for you *(John 3: 16)*.

Reflection

Seek out healing for your self-image before you start dating again. If you don't have a sense of personal worth, it will be easy to seek a guy's attention in order to feel special and desirable again, making you an easy target for mistreatment. Meditating on the promises above will help you appreciate your value in God's eyes. He also wants you to build an album of memories of His love in action. What incidences can you recall of how God has shown His special care? This week, ask God to show you and remind you that you are His special girl.

Prayer

Dear Lord, You loved me enough to send Your Son to die for me. Your word tells me over and over again how precious I am in Your sight and how much You love me. O Lord, I give my shattered self to You. I think so little of myself and have sold out many times just to feel important! Lord, thank You for hearing my prayer and restoring my significance and worth!

Take your needs to God

The Lord despises double standards of every kind. (Proverbs 20: 10)

The godly know the rights of the poor; the wicked don't care to know. (Proverbs 29: 7)

At one point in my life, I didn't put much worth or value on my needs. I didn't see myself as an equal to men and treated them better than I treated myself. For example, I would cook steak for my partner while I made an economy meal for myself. If he disappeared from our home for a week, I didn't feel I had the right to question him, but if I was not at home when he returned, I would be in the wrong. He had the right to be angry, but I did not. He had the right to inquire about what I did without him, but what he did was none of my business. It was surprisingly easy to put up with offensive behaviour and I gave my partner greater privileges and freedoms than I allowed myself, because I didn't feel I had the right to ask him to treat me respectfully.

Though I didn't feel equal to men, I learned that the Lord does not show more favour to men than to women. He does not intend for men to wield power over women, forcing them into a subservient role. In fact, the Bible instructs men to *'be good husbands to your wives. Honour them, delight in them. As women they lack some of your advantages. But in the new life of God's grace, you're equals. Treat your wives, then, as equals so your prayers don't run aground' (1 Peter 3: 7 MSG; see also Galatians 3: 28).* After discovering this truth in God's word, I began to see that I was wrong to think that men had a right to treat me harshly. As I started to understand my importance in God's eyes, I learned how to acknowledge and reject disrespectful behaviour without feeling guilty.

My eyes were opened to the equal importance of my own needs, and the wonderful truth that I could go confidently to God, expecting Him to meet them. God's promise says that He will *'supply all your needs from his glorious riches, which have been given to us in Christ Jesus' (Philippians 4: 19).* The fact that Jesus can see my needs and fills my life with good things has freed me from the guilt I had about asking Him for anything.

Today, I no longer neglect my needs or put men on a pedestal. I can recognise men who respect women and show consideration for the thoughts and feelings of others and I have learned to assert my needs to others. At one time, the type of men I was with would have accused me of being unreasonable or too demanding for thinking this way but that attitude no longer shames me into silent submission. In fact, the word teaches us that love makes requirements and encourages us to make our requests known to God, for He delights in giving us His support and showing us His amazing power and strength!

Others may have stripped you of your rights but those experiences don't prove you are worthless. The way they have treated you has not gained God's approval. His heart is with those who have been oppressed and to reinstate their rights. He says' This is what the LORD says: Do what is just and right. Rescue from the hand of his oppressor the one who has been robbed. Do no wrong or violence to the alien, the fatherless or the widow, and do not shed innocent blood in this place. *Jeremiah 22: 3.* Be comforted. Your God has given you worth and knows your needs even before you ask Him, so why continue to believe that you cannot go to Him in faith making your requests known to Him?

Reflection

Does your partner have unfair and unreasonable expectations, making your relationship revolve around his demands? Are you devoting yourself to catering to your man's needs, even if that means neglecting your own? In most cases, adapting your behaviour in an effort to satisfy a man's demands is futile; it is more likely that he will only keep demanding more from you.

God recognises you have needs and promises to meet them. What disappointments and neglected needs can you bring to God? Remember, you can speak to God anytime, anywhere.

Also make it a daily practice to take responsibility for your needs and set small goals to help you achieve this (i.e. ask for what you need, take a class, make time for friends, go to the gym, find some time alone to think, say no and do the right thing). Remember, making requirements and setting limits on unreasonable demands is not selfishness but part of experiencing safe relationships.

Prayer

I don't always feel like I have the right to ask for what I need, but I know that You care about me, Lord, and that knowledge gives me the courage to come to You and seek Your blessings. Thank You for loving me and knowing what I need even before I ask.

*See the segment titled 'Basic rights and needs' for more information on this topic.

Heal your feelings towards men

Jesus said, *'Father, forgive these people, because they don't know what they are doing.' (Luke 23: 34)*

My best friend can still vividly recall the day I hid behind her big couch cushions when she mentioned the word 'men'!
I remember, too. I liked her husband and a few other men from church, but that was all. The rest of the 'male species' made me recoil. I hated and feared men. I thought I would never want anything to do with them again.

The thought of allowing a man access to my heart and my trust inspired coldness and fear within me. I believed that all men, no matter how nice they appeared were basically all the same and could not be trusted.

Watching how my best friend's husband treated her challenged my thinking. I saw that some men in the church really loved their wives, which was something I was not used to and thought a bit strange. I also met a few who did not treat their wives so well. Those were the ones I understood the most, and their actions helped justify my reasons for staying aloof.

Over time, I began to see that not all men were the same. I also began to think about my behaviour and how cold and shut-off I had become. My mistrust of men affected my ability to feel a part of a church. I started to see that hurting people hurt others and that my icy exterior was keeping good people locked out of my life. Recognising my behaviour helped me gain a different perspective towards the men from my past relationships, as I realised how much we all needed God to heal us and help us stop hurting one another.

Many women hate men and at the same time strongly desire to meet a man that loves them. As I struggled with these mixed emotions, I began to see that it was impossible to love a man when I hated all men in general. I needed to forgive and release the guys from my past, not so I could be free to date again, but so I could be free from hatred and passing judgement on every man I met.

Learning to forgive the men that have hurt you in your past is like healing ointment for your soul. While you hold on to your resentment, you give your past the power to mould your life today. Hatred will breed suspicion within you and will lead to all sorts of defence behaviours, arguments, relationship breakdowns, and wrong choices in love.

Having learned to forgive, I no longer hide behind cushions. I am free to enjoy the company of men without fearing their motives or worrying that they will hurt me in some way. When you learn to let go and forgive, you won't have to hide behind cushions anymore, either.

Reflection

Have you built a defensive barrier around your heart? What is this barrier protecting you from? Do you love and yet hate men at the same time? What are you holding on to that confession, healing, and forgiveness would release you from?

Prayer

Dear Lord, I want to work through my issues with men and identify the reasons I have these bitter, angry, and hateful feelings inside. I come to You with my pain and ask that You will walk me down the road that leads to healing and forgiveness. I don't want my past to ruin my future.

Loneliness doesn't need a date

I am like an owl in the desert, like a lonely owl in a far-off wilderness. I lie awake, lonely as a solitary bird on the roof. (Psalm 102: 6–7)

I had been single for a couple of years. I was enjoying my new relationship with Christ, absorbing the peace and quiet after such a chaotic past and relishing in all God's blessings.

Around this time, I developed an attraction toward someone from my church. We had become friends and I was secretly hoping it would blossom into something more. I thought my hopes were going to be realised one day, when he called to say he had something important to share with me. I held my breath as he fumbled shyly to speak his feelings. He said he wanted me to be the first to know he had finally met the woman of his dreams – but he wasn't referring to me! I fought quite an emotional battle to keep my composure and refrain from bursting into tears!

Watching the new couple together provoked feelings of rejection within me. As I wrestled with my emotions, I asked the Lord to show me why I felt so hurt by the actions of a man I'd never dated. Straight away He answered, telling me that I was very lonely and that my hurt feelings were not entirely connected to this man. Over the coming months, I went through a season of experiences designed to show me just how isolated I had become.

I craved a sense of belonging and desired to find a place in this big wide world that I could fit into. I always felt different from others and in many ways I was still detaching myself from people because of my insecurities. As I shared my feelings with the Lord, He gently removed the attraction I had developed for my friend and showed me that another dating relationship wasn't what I really needed at that time.

In the past, loneliness would have sent me straight to the nearest club, looking for a new boyfriend. I thought being with anyone was better than being lonely, and if I couldn't find a man to fill the void, I would drown out the emptiness with drink. Without these crutches to turn to, I was forced to face the real issue: I found being close to others painful. After a long process, I've found a group of people I can feel safe with. I now understand that I can't cure loneliness by finding another lover.

Dating offers us the chance to meet new people and find the right partner, but intense loneliness has to be addressed at a much deeper level. If you feel lonely and isolated, use your emptiness as a pathway to draw closer to God and discover how you can feel part of a community again. The Lord's desire is to set you in a family (Psalm 68: 6); be open to whatever ways God provides this family, for He knows what it is you really need.

Reflection

Have you tried to end loneliness by looking for Mr. Right? Unchecked loneliness leads to desperate choices. The Lord does not want you to choose someone out of fear of being alone or because you are desperately lonely. He has dealt with all our issues on the cross. He can heal the intense pain and emptiness in your heart, if you open it up to Him.

Prayer

Dear Jesus, Your word says that You will never leave nor forsake me. Please grant me a revelation of Your nearness. Fill the empty, lonely parts of me and guide me to a community of people with whom I can experience a sense of belonging and connection.

Be seen and heard

I prayed to the Lord, and he answered me, freeing me from all my fears. Those who look to him for help will be radiant with joy; no shadow of shame will darken their faces. I cried out to the Lord in my suffering, and he heard me. He set me free from all my fears. *(Psalm 34: 4–6)*

My father used to say that children should be seen and not heard. As a child, I took his words to heart and when the time came to develop relationships of my own, I found I couldn't open up without intense difficulty and feelings of unworthiness.

Deep inside I had a hungering desire to be heard, but I hid my true thoughts and feelings. Instead, I gravitated toward partners who were poor listeners and more interested in their own needs than mine. My attempts to communicate led to the same type of complaints:

I spoke to you, and I never received a helpful response.

I looked to you for reassurance, but I was not comforted.

I shared what was on my heart, and I walked away ashamed.

I asked you for what I needed, but the experience was not good.

I never really knew what it was like to be heard until I entered a relationship with Jesus. I can't recall how many times I cried during prayer because I felt so deeply understood by Him. Being fully known by Christ has healed many of my insecurities, low self-esteem, and shame. *Psalm 34: 4–5*, aptly summarises what being heard by God has felt like for me:

Verse 4 I spoke to the Lord, and He answered me. (You gave me a helpful response.)

Verse 4 He freed me from all my fears. (You gave me reassurance.)

Verse 5 No shadow of shame has darkened my face. (I didn't feel ashamed coming to You.)

Verse 5 I felt joy when I looked to Him for help. (It was a good experience talking with You.)

The old me has now been replaced with the new me in Christ. I no longer see myself as unworthy of an equal relationship in which each partner listens and considers the other's feelings; I now understand that this type of exchange is part of a normal, healthy relationship.

If you have lived as one who is seen and not heard, discover for yourself the pure joy of talking with God. His listening ear is guaranteed to heal the unheard parts of you.

Reflection

Is there a part of you that feels unseen and unheard? God longs to lavish His love and concern upon you. He always has time to listen to you and longs to answer your prayers.

Prayer

Lord, I want to experience the satisfaction of being both seen and heard. I accept Your invitation to talk to You, so that You can fulfil your promise to restore the parts of me that feel unnoticed.

Stop waiting to be rescued

If you wait for perfect conditions, you will never get anything done. (Ecclesiastes 11: 4)

I seated myself amongst the dry, hot grass at the back of our holiday resort, staring at the mountains on the Island of Corfu in Greece. I could hardly believe what I saw. Having lived my entire life in London, this was the first time I had ever seen such beautiful views. The experience was even more special because the Lord had told me just a few weeks earlier that He wanted to take me to Greece. Though I didn't have the money, He somehow made a way for me and my mother to go.

As I silently admired the picturesque view, a part of my soul opened up. I awakened to a new level of understanding about God and the person He made me. I was not just a city girl, but a woman who loved and appreciated the mountains and seacoast. How I loved to explore! I discovered an adventurous side of myself and booked our week with cruises, speedboats, exploration swims amongst the caves, cool dips in the lagoons, food at fine restaurants, and lazy hours browning our overly white skin!

These new experiences contrasted greatly with the life I had lived before going on the trip. I had spent most of my time focusing on men and seeking a knight in shining armour to give me an exciting life. Nothing was more important than sorting this out first and as a result I was unfulfilled, bored, and resentful towards those who did well. It never crossed my mind to act on any of the dreams in my heart because they never seemed possible or desirable without the right man to share them with. I was used to living with very little, expecting very little, and having very little as a result.

Since my time in Greece, the Lord has taken me on other short trips and much further abroad. Through these experiences, God has provided many chances to deepen my faith, furtherance of my academic education, life lessons, and development of my character. I have outgrown the woman that never expected much or ventured into new things.

Your walk with the Lord may not lead you on trips around the globe. He may have other kinds of adventures in store for you. If you are waiting for a knight in shining armour to appear before you start living the life God intends, you will miss His amazing blessings right here in the now.

Following God opens your life to the possibility of greater adventures than you could ever imagine. You will realise the dreams He has put in your heart, because nothing will be impossible for you through Him. You can make new friends, proclaim God's goodness, take that job offer, start a business, go to school, or start a ministry and have a full life right now. By living today, you are not forfeiting the possibility of meeting the right guy or being married one day.

Overcome your fear of being single and do the things God has put on your heart. Quit thinking that finding your knight is all that matters. God has called you to be a messenger of His saving power. He delights in seeing a smile on your face and watching you enjoy life. God had planned for you to do mighty things: *'The truth is, anyone who believes in me will do the same works I have done, and even greater works, because I am going to be with the Father. You can ask for anything in my name, and I will do it, because the work of the Son brings glory to the Father. Yes, ask anything in my name, and I will do it' (John 14: 12–14).*

God has promised you a new life that doesn't begin in heaven; it starts now! Ask Jesus to be your knight in shining armour, for He is the only one that can give you all the desires of your heart!

Reflection

Have you been waiting for a husband instead of living your life today? What things have you put on hold because you want to be married first? Rather than waiting for married life, how might Ephesians 5: 15–17 encourage you to make the most of today?

Prayer

Dear Lord, I am not happy with my single life and want a way out. Rather than waiting to see what a man can give me, help me live a full life now so I can contribute to a relationship. Help me to enjoy my life in all circumstances and trust that You will take care of my future.

Give up the fantasy

*For the weapons of our warfare are not of the flesh, but mighty
before God to the casting down of strongholds, casting down
imaginations, and every high thing that is exalted against the
knowledge of God, and bringing every thought into captivity to the
obedience of Christ. (2 Corinthians 10: 5 ASV)*

He was the new boy in school; the one I fell in love with at first
sight. He was the first real love of my life. We shared special
dates, stolen kisses, and promises of love. He was the only one
on my mind and he held my heart in a special way. Of course,
we never spoke to one another; in fact, I don't think he even
noticed me at school! Our entire relationship took place in the
realm of my imagination. Our fictional love affair started in
my mind, based on what I thought it might be like to be with
him—and how wonderfully we got along!

Fantasising encouraged false ideas about love, and by the
time I eventually started to date, I had developed very high
expectations. Each time I left my date's side, I daydreamed about
what it would be like when we saw each other again. I was so
starry-eyed that I could see no flaws in him or obstacles blocking
the progress of our relationship.

Devastation set in when the honeymoon period gave way to
reality! I viewed everything my boyfriend did differently or less
often as a sign that his feelings were changing and that I was
not good enough for him. Each change made me try all the
more to get back to the way things were.

Obsessively dreaming about finding the perfect man
drastically affects our expectations in a real relationship! If we
are desperate for love we will deny or overlook anything that
doesn't seem right, in order to protect the dream we want to

come true. What we really hold on to, however, is the fantasy, not the man.

One key to freedom is learning about the difference between infatuation and love, a difference Paul talks about in 1 Corinthians 13. Infatuation relies on feelings and is a temporary shallow longing, while real love involves commitment, loyalty, and faithfulness. Infatuation focuses on what it can gain from another person while real love gives unselfishly, in the best interests of the other person. These truths are important to consider; when we focus on meeting the perfect man in order to make us feel better, we are really thinking about what we can get rather than what we can give in a relationship.

God showed me that my dream man was such a vision of perfection that I would never meet him on planet earth! I surrendered my fantasies because I no longer wanted to be guided by false images, created during a time I was desperately searching for love. I have learnt to bring myself back to the real world by prayerfully asking the Holy Spirit to guide me and allow facts to determine the course of my dating life.

If you want to have something real, give God your false ideas and images about love. Leave your ideas about the perfect man at the foot of the cross because he doesn't exist in the real world. Thank God for His love and let Him know that you trust Him enough to give you everything you need in life. You can be sure that as you seek the Lord for wisdom and guidance, He will protect you from searching for the right life partner based on a figment of your imagination!

Reflection

Is your understanding of love built upon the excitement and passion of a new relationship? Have you made long-term commitments based on how things feel in the beginning? What happened? What fantasies do you have about romance and love? Would you be willing to give these false ideas to God? This week, ask the Holy Spirit to show you your misconceptions about love. He will help you learn to remove any false imaginations from your mind.

Prayer

Dear Lord, I rush in with my heart, hoping all my expectations and desires for love will be satisfied. In my haste, my dreams for love have often failed. I am ready to learn about true love, Lord. It is something I have always wanted to experience. Please help me to feel loved by You and know what real love is truly all about.

Face your fears

O God, I praise your word. I trust in God, so why should I be afraid?
What can mere mortals do to me? (Psalm 56: 4)

I had left the comfort of my familiar surroundings in London and travelled to Canada to learn how to be a Life Skills Coach. As I sat in group one day, we were told that we were going to do a session on anger. Straight away, I felt fear rising within me. I ran from the classroom crying, saying 'I don't do anger!' As far as I was concerned, I wanted nothing more to do with angry people and I didn't like the fact that I was going to have to work on such a painful subject.

I eventually went back to the group and told them why I ran out. Thankfully, I had some very wise coaches who taught me how to deal with anger instead of running away. As uncomfortable as it was for me, I learnt that I didn't have to run any more. The Lord showed me that He had removed a lot of bad things from my life, but there were still some things I had to grow beyond. By the time I left the course, I was able to work as a Life Skills Coach with women in recovery from drug addiction and abuse. I learned how to help these women work through their anger without running away from them.

I have come to understand that God often leads us through situations, rather than remove them, so that we can face the things we think will be too painful or frightening for us to handle. We often make these predictions because of past experiences, but when we face trials with God, going through them in His strength and His way, the outcomes turn out very differently. If we don't learn to walk with God through these times, we will keep giving up and quitting too soon, never understanding how to work through issues and build solid, intimate relationships.

The longer you run from your past and your fears, the longer it will take you to experience new things. *Proverbs 28: 1* tells us that those who don't know God run away from things when nothing is chasing them, but people who trust God are as bold as lions. God helps us to become bold and courageous, no longer fearing people and what they might do to us.

Breathe faith into your thinking and become more consciously aware of how many things God is doing differently in your life today. Embrace the challenges ahead of you and rejoice that God is at work within you, daily helping you experience the new life He has given you.

Reflection

Learning new relationship skills is vitally important to developing healthier relationships. What skills do you need to develop? What parts of your past still haunts you and makes you fear learning how to cope with relationship challenges? In what ways can you remind yourself that you have been given a new life? What promises of God can you hold on to while you face and overcome your fears?

Prayer

Dear Lord, I fear my past because _____. Please release me from my fears. Inspire me with new thoughts, so I can begin the process of changing how I think about my past and my current situations.

Recover from your past

Yet now he has brought you back as his friends. He has done this through his death on the cross in his own human body. As a result, he has brought you into the very presence of God, and you are holy and blameless as you stand before him without a single fault. (Colossians 1: 22)

When I became a Christian, I knew that God loved and accepted me, but I harboured deep fears about how I was going to be viewed by Christian men who I assumed would only want to date a woman without a history like mine.

I used to wonder if any of them would understand me and would he lose interest once he knew my background. I felt ashamed of and less confident of what I could expect from the Lord and less hopeful about the promises He had given me. However, instead of addressing my presumptuous fear, I buried it inside.

In my earlier efforts at dating, this fear came to life. I worried that each man would ask awkward questions about my past, so I reasoned that if I told him up front about my past and he accepted it, I could relax! However, being so open so soon was not the way to build a healthy relationship. I did not know these men and it was my responsibility to guard my heart and not share too much too soon. In one instance, my direct approach proved dangerous as my openness was used against me later on.

My sense of shame indicated that a part of me still held on to old insecurities and I was still hiding from people. I took my fears and shame to God and now I hold a very different attitude about my past and do not fear what other people think of me.

Shame causes us to hide and not come into God's presence for healing. It keeps us locked in the dark feeling condemned, dirty and unwanted. This is not coming from God as His love draws us out of the dark so we can be healed and be put into a right relationship with Him, forgiven and cleansed.

If you feel ashamed because of your past and are attempting to date, take a step back for a while and address how you feel with God. He wants you to know that there is absolutely no truth behind your fear of never being loved or accepted because of your past! To believe such a lie is to believe that God can't love you and that there is no place for God's chosen ones to belong in His family.

He wants you to enjoy being a new creation in Christ, forgiven, accepted, and loved. So take to Him whatever is causing you shame and as He heals, you will be able to believe in your new identity in Christ.

Don't let your past dictate your identity anymore. Jesus died that you might have a new life and your transformation from the past is now your testimony! Let the light of Christ dwelling in your shine brightly for all to see!

Reflection

How does shame affect you? How does it cause you to act and behave? As loved and accepted women of God, we take comfort in knowing that we also have His approval and can take our shameful feelings to Him for healing.

Prayer

Dear Lord, heal my shame. I want to be free to live for today and embrace the new life You have given me. Thank You for covering my past with Your righteousness and giving me a new start.

Don't seek revenge

Dear Friends, never avenge yourselves. Leave that to God. For it is written, 'I will take vengeance; I will repay those who deserve it' says the Lord. (Romans 12: 19)

I once read that abuse creates debts, and I believe this to be correct. Abusive people take and do not give; they rob people of their rights and do not show compassion or repentance. They believe that they have the right to behave the way they do, and because they gain 'rewards' with little cost, they are often very resistant to change. Think about the man who treats his partner like a servant or controls her every move. To 'pay her back' would require becoming responsible, treating her as an equal, giving her his trust, and letting her have independent thought and action that might not fall in line with his desires.

A victim's desire for justice is natural. But if this desire is left unchecked, it can fester into angry, revengeful thoughts that keep her locked in the past. This happened to me when a relationship ended in a way that hurt me very deeply. Almost a year later, I was still replaying the hurtful memories. My sense of justice wanted payback and I found myself creating imaginary arguments with my ex in order to finally receive the respect and remorse I felt he owed me.

God showed me that my ex-boyfriend would be living with his debts until he repented and sought change. It was not my place to burden myself with constant reminders of what he 'owed' me, nor was it my job to get payback, even if only in my thoughts. Instead, I was asked to place my pain and my ex's unpaid debts into God's hands, letting Him heal me and fulfil His promise to repay the losses suffered.

By forgiving my ex and releasing him from his debts, I also stopped myself from developing a defensive barrier around my heart, living in fear of being treated the same way again. I could now step out of that fear and focus on my own issues rather than his.

Let us learn from how God deals with offences. When His children do wrong, He calls them to repentance and chooses to forgive and rebuild His relationship with them. He does not hold onto offences and because His Son has paid for our debts, He makes us faultless and without blame in His presence. Regarding His enemies; He does not allow their behaviour to alter His character. He continues to do what is right, just and fair and this is how He overcomes evil.

As you continue to acknowledge and work through how people have mistreated you, keep your mind and soul free from further damage by wanting revenge. Your offender belongs to God and He will do what is right for that person's life; he is no longer your concern.

Forgiving your offender does not mean you are allowing him to 'get away' with what he has done or that you have to bring him back into your life. Forgiveness allows you to stop subjecting yourself to further abuse or pain as you replay the memories and allows you to let go so that you can move on and focus on God's plan for your life.

Reflection

Do you have a catalogue of memories that incite hatred and revengeful thoughts? Memories such as these need the soothing balm of God's healing love. Bring your hurts to him and be willing to let go of your desire for revenge. Even if you don't feel like you want to let go, your openness before God will allow Him to take you on a journey of healing, freeing you from constantly reliving the past.

Prayer

I have wanted _____ to know how much he has hurt me and to feel some of my pain. The memories still haunt me, but I don't want to live this way, God. I want to be free and find joy in life again. Thank You for caring so much about the injustices in my life. I am grateful that I don't have to take care of this anymore. I leave my tangled past in Your hands and I am willing to find new life again in You.

Do things differently

Trust in the Lord with all your heart; do not depend on your own understanding. Seek his will in all you do, and he will direct your paths. (Proverbs 3: 5–6)

I wasn't sure what was going on in his heart; He was physically present, but he seemed emotionally cold and distant. He said everything was fine between us, but I wasn't convinced. I prayed that God would show me what was wrong—and He did.

By the end of the day, my date confessed that he didn't believe I was the right one for him. He had seemed distant because he wasn't sure how to tell me. Though I was disappointed, I was relieved to know the truth. However, the very next day he developed a change of heart. He said he feared that at some point in the future he would realise he was making a mistake, and he asked if I would wait for him.

When he asked me to wait, I felt a familiar happiness and relief well up inside me, and out of my mouth popped a yes! My enthusiasm lasted for about ten minutes, until I sensed the Lord gently prompting me to think about my answer.

The Lord wanted me to understand that when a man decided I was not the right one for him, I should not allow myself to be put in the background in case he changed his mind. He said it is not good to give to a double-minded person *(James 1: 5–8)* and by waiting, I was not putting into action what He had taught me. In the past, I would have waited for a guy that 'didn't want me, but didn't want to be without me' to my own detriment. God wanted me to pay closer attention to what I was looking for in a man, and let those values guide my decisions.

I now understand why I initially said I would wait. I did not know how to handle disappointment and I was used to waiting and hoping to be loved. This man's rejection was a reminder of how I had grown used to feeling unlovable; I started to cry and behave as if the world was coming to an end! I still had a lot of learning to do about God's unfailing love, unlimited goodness, and kindness towards me. The Lord had not pulled down the curtain on my life; there was certainly no need for me to do it! I had God's assurance that there were still many blessings to claim and more adventures up ahead and I knew he wanted me to get up from this place, thanking Him for the lessons learnt.

A year later, I looked back on the experience with new eyes. The Lord certainly is a kind and loving God. He taught me what the right course of action was to take that day. He taught me to respect myself more. He showed me that it is better to experience a moment of disappointment than stay with someone who didn't really want to be with me.

Perhaps you are not very good at dealing with loss and don't like going through the pain of disappointment. Sometimes our disappointments can be our biggest blessings because they prepare the way for us to receive something better. Don't miss out on God's best for you. Trust God to use your disappointments to lead you where He wants you to be.

Reflection

Do disappointments in love crush you? Do you find it difficult to move on? Are you focused on a previous disappointment in your dating life and too afraid to try again? God is a God of new beginnings and fresh starts. If you give Him a chance, He will help you recover from your latest disappointment.

Prayer

Dear Lord, though I strain to see it now, I trust that You care about my life and that, in time, You will use my disappointments to bless me in some way. Thank You for taking my tough times and using them to bring about better things for me.

Be guided by peace

*'Go out and stand before me on the mountain,' the Lord told
him. And as Elijah stood there, the Lord passed by, and a mighty
windstorm hit the mountain. It was such a terrible blast that the
rocks were torn loose, but the Lord was not in the wind. After
the wind there was an earthquake, but the Lord was not in the
earthquake. And after the earthquake there was a fire, but the Lord
was not in the fire. And after the fire there was the sound of a gentle
whisper. (1 Kings 19: 11–12)*

We had been dating for a couple of months, but I was starting
to feel a lack of peace when we were together. I couldn't readily
pinpoint anything in his character that would cause me to feel
uneasy, so one Friday night I prayed for guidance. I heard God
reply that over the weekend He would reveal the cause of my
inner disturbance.

The following day I felt anxious, unsure of what the next few
hours might bring. By the end of the afternoon, I discovered
that my boyfriend had been hiding an addiction problem and
that he was not ready to seek the Lord for help.

Looking over relationships that were not right for me, I can
clearly remember when the warning bells went off inside.
My habit had been to ignore my gut feelings and keep going
forward. Finally, I have learned to listen, viewing these inner
promptings as a gentle warning from God that I had wandered
off His path somewhere. As I have grown and developed trust
in Him, I question and resist Him less. I have a greater desire to
heed to the Lord's still small voice and follow the path of peace.

Our God knows everything. When He whispers to our hearts,
we do not need to know all the details of His plan, even if
obedience to His commands doesn't fit in with our desires. God

studies the hearts and motivations of every human being and knows how to guide us to the best companions. All we need to do is develop a willingness to listen and a desire to find our way back on the right path again.

This is a wonderful assurance for those of you who fear relationships: God is right beside you, leading the way. The next time you don't feel quite right about dating someone, it is safer to acknowledge your feelings and explore them rather than ignore your conscience and have no peace in your relationship. You can trust that God is not trying to spoil your chances of finding happiness. He just loves you so much that He wants to move you in the right direction and give you His best.

Reflection

Learning to be confident about your intuition or convictions can take time, especially if you have learned to ignore them due to how you were taught to behave or because of hurtful repercussions. God is no dictator. He will not force you to follow Him, but will gently lead you. Listen for His quiet voice and follow the path that gives you a sense of right doing and peace.

Prayer

Lord, teach me to trust my inner convictions instead of pushing them aside. Help me not to doubt my judgements and intuition or hold onto something that is a lie or not the best You have for me. Create in me a pure and obedient heart, so that I when I hear your voice, I follow.

Celebrate change

I don't mean to say that I have already achieved these things or that I have already reached perfection! But I keep working toward that day when I will finally be all that Christ Jesus saved me for and wants me to be. (Philippians 3: 12)

When I started dating again, I thought that I was ready and that I would not continue to repeat past mistakes. I was stepping out with God beside me and was not going it alone without Him. I believed that everything would be different this time!

However, some of my new dating experiences brought out areas in me that still required healing, but Jesus showed me that I should not beat myself up for not being where I thought I should be. It was an opportunity to keep waiting upon God as I addressed the areas with Him that I was still weak in.

Becoming more like Christ takes time. God is not in a rush to make us more like His son. Our part is to stay close to God and keep seeking wisdom and understanding about how to build healthy relationships. The journey, however, is well worth the time it takes. God helped me gain a positive attitude and see that I have many reasons to praise His name, because through Him I had overcome many situations that would have defeated me in the past.

If you have stepped out and have made mistakes, maintain a godly attitude and become teachable rather than miserable. As long as you are walking in the guidance of the Holy Spirit and submitting your life to God, you can rest assured that you have His forgiveness and help.

Look through the following list of changes that you want to be striving towards in your relationships. May these examples serve as an encouraging reminder to you of how you are moving forward on the right path:

- God has become your fulfilment and your joy.
- Your relationship with Jesus is not lost when you date.
- You may accept a date with the wrong type of man, but recognise it and move on.
- You are more aware of how you feel. You don't dismiss uneasy feelings, but address what makes you feel that way.
- You speak what is on your mind without feeling guilty about your honesty.
- You are honest with yourself rather than going into denial, hoping things will get better.
- You are willing to give the man who appears 'not your type' a chance and find out more about him.
- You no longer excuse abusive behaviour.
- You see that you can do things by yourself without waiting to find a husband first.
- You enjoy your own company.
- You still see your friends when you are dating.
- You realise you are not so focused on romantic feelings, but are more concerned about what a man is really like as a person.
- You start to confront problems instead of ignoring their existence.
- You feel comfortable being yourself and no longer think that you have to change in order to be accepted.
- You are not bored and lonely without a boyfriend. You find you are busy with your own life.
- You start to recognise ungodly behaviour before you get involved.
- You are waiting for marriage to enjoy a sexual relationship.
- You don't need charm and flattery to feel good about yourself.
- You no longer hate your life and wish that you had a man to make you feel better.

- You start to involve other people in your dating life and don't isolate away from them.
- You are not afraid to assert your values and say no to someone.
- Your mind is not frantically filled with fear and negative thoughts about being abandoned, disliked, or rejected. You have peace and feel secure.

Reflection

Keep a diary of your growth in relationships. Use this journal to encourage yourself as you grow. Remember to thank God for any changes and rejoice that the Lord is healing your life!

Prayer

Dear Lord, I want to thank You that though I am not yet where I want to be, I am changing into the woman You created me to be. I give You thanks and praise for changing _____ about me and I am committed to staying with You and letting You make me the woman You want me to be!

Stay faithful in all circumstances

The Lord will work out his plans for my life. (Psalm 138: 8)

So you decided to trust God with your dating life, gave up men that didn't know Him, and met a man that you thought had God's approval.

Your friends think he is a God-send and you are fairly convinced the relationship is going to go the whole way. Suddenly, things begin to unravel and before you know it, everything between you has come to an end.

This scenario happened to me and I have listened to other Christian women share similar experiences. Responses vary; some have become angry and bitter with God asking why He allowed them to meet the man. Others feared God was forcing them to remain single forever and some found their way into a new understanding of God working things out on their behalf. How have you responded when you thought you had God's approval but He said no?

I have come to understand that the Lord will not prevent us from going through a break-up, but this is not a reason to push Him away or let that be the deciding factor on how greatly we trust Him. Our relationship with Jesus goes deeper than our circumstances and we need to know that He is in control despite how hurt we feel.

After a break-up, stay connected with God; run to Him rather than from Him. While you talk to Him, He will comfort you and gather your tears in His bottle. *(Psalm 56: 8).* He will then give you His understanding of the matter. You may discover that you missed something about your man's character and God, in His kindness, remembered His promise to protect you *(Psalm 18: 2).* Perhaps this man came into your life only for a season to fulfil some part of God's restoration plan for you both or God has yet to give you His best.

Whatever you discover, don't allow your frustration to push you out of God's loving arms. If you are patient, you will shine all the more brightly for having been through this life experience. Give God a chance to do His thing. Though you may be hurt and angry that this particular relationship didn't work out, be encouraged that God will fulfil His plans, purposes, and promises for your life.

God has promised that you will reap the desires of your heart if you stay faithful. Believe in the One who loved you enough to die for you and in time you will see the difference in how you perceive things now.

Reflection

Are you learning to trust God no matter what you are going through or has a break up hampered your faith? Sometimes we are so focused on everything that went wrong that we can't see what good we can take from our experiences. The Lord's care for you comes from a true heart (Psalm 78: 72). Waiting upon the Lord will open a way for you to gain God's understanding, for His thinking and ways are different than ours (Isaiah 55: 8–9).

Prayer

Dear Lord, I sometimes take my disappointments out on You, but You are not the enemy. You are my friend! I need You, God. Help me trust that You love me and that You are working even this disappointment out for my good.

Don't compromise

Don't team up with those who are unbelievers. (2 Corinthians 6: 14)

The most important thing in my life is the relationship I have with Jesus. I could not imagine a life without Him and I do not know how I would cope without having His strong arm to lean on. He is someone with whom I can share my deepest thoughts – the Man I can come to for advice, who comforts my heart and teaches me how to live successfully. If anyone really wants to know who I am and what I stand for, they will discover that my spiritual walk is the first priority in my life. When it comes to involving my heart with a man, I need to know that Christ is at the centre of his life, too.

Some women, discouraged by the lack of available single men in the church, get tired of waiting and settle for a man of no faith rather than have no man at all. If you are thinking of committing your heart to a man who is not a believer, though the attraction might be very strong and you have a lot of things in common, there are some things worth considering before you tie the knot.

Your heart's connection with Christ is the deepest part of you. How will you feel about never being able to have a spiritual connection with your husband? What would happen when a pressing problem arose? Will that mean that you will be alone in your prayer life, seeking the Lord for guidance and answers? When the storms of life hit, when the odds seem stacked against you and your faith is tested, will you be taking faith action while your husband's unbelief will be guiding his actions? When you attend church, pray, and build friendships with other believers, will you be on your own while he is at home, working, or out playing sports?

What will happen if you decide to have a child? Will Christian values and beliefs be modelled and taught in your home or will your child learn to live by whatever standard feels right to your husband? When you have moments of spiritual breakthrough and enjoy wonderful experiences with the Lord, will you have to keep them to yourself because your husband cannot identify with or understand spiritual things *(1 Corinthians 2: 14)*?

These are just a few questions to think about, but the message is clear. You might be lonely and tired of waiting for the right man, but if you compromise now, you will be even lonelier when romance has been replaced by the rigors of daily life.

The Lord is not trying to rob you of happiness and lead you into a monastic life. He is helping you avoid a life filled with difficulty and the possibility of compromising your relationship with Him because of a partner's unbelief. He does not want you to experience another painful love.

It is far better to be lonely and single than lonely and married. My prayer is that you will believe in the Lord's unfailing love and that, if you choose to be married, you will be united with someone who shares your love for the Lord, for that kind of union will bring great rewards: *'How happy are those who fear the Lord—all who follow his ways! You will enjoy the fruit of your labour. How happy you will be! How rich your life' (Psalm 128: 1–2).*

Reflection

Have you been waiting a long time to meet a man of faith? Do you maintain hope or are you harbouring feelings of anger, bitterness, and disappointment? How do you deal with these feelings? Have you compromised and convinced yourself that it won't hurt your walk with God to marry an unbeliever? What are the costs of doing things your way? What are the benefits of choosing God's way?

Prayer

Dear Lord, it is hard saying no when I am attracted to men that don't know You. I know I would be entertaining a love that would have its problems later on down the road. Right now Lord, I need Your help to do the right thing and stay on the path You have chosen. You have promised me help and that I will be rewarded. I love You and accept Your way, for it is the best path for me.

Become a whole woman

Wait patiently for the Lord. Be brave and courageous. Yes, wait patiently for the Lord. Psalm 27: 14

During the summer of 2005, the Lord led me to start a counselling, coaching, and training service called Donna Intera, which is an Italian term for 'whole woman'. The vision the Lord gave me was to minister to and educate women on the importance of becoming whole women so that they can be attracted to and build healthy relationships with men who are also whole.

At the same time, I was still working out this vision in my own life. I had been dating in the hope of forming a serious relationship and as much as I had grown and changed my behaviours and choices showed me that there were still parts of me that were not yet ready.

The Lord wanted me to continue to use my singleness as a time of becoming whole and while that wait has been frustrating at times, I have seen the transformation taking place. This period has been much longer than I expected it to be and if I had given up waiting and chose to do things independently, I might now be married . . . but not to the right man.

It is easy to grumble and complain during the waiting season, but that's not the attitude God wants you and I to adopt. He wants our words to be filled with faith, hope, and expectancy that He will bring about the desires of our heart as we commit ourselves to His timing and ways first. The word says *'He will give you all you need from day to day if you live for him and make the Kingdom of God your primary concern' (Mathew 6: 33).*

We can always find a man, but in order to receive the man with God's favour we must be ready and prepared. This means we keep our eyes on the Lord and obediently follow. The word instructs us to *'notice the way God does things; then fall into line'* *(Ecclesiastes 7: 13).*

It is a sobering thought that we can also forfeit God's blessing by stubbornly resisting His promptings and leadings, remaining unwilling to change, or allowing ourselves to be ruled by doubt and settling for someone we know is not the right one.

If you want God's best, be the person who is ready and therefore able to receive His blessing. The Lord has promised many good gifts to those who love and trust Him and promises that no sorrow comes with His gifts *(Proverbs 10: 22).* When we do life God's way, we can happily look ahead knowing that the gift of marriage will be given with joy and not pain. Our hearts will be able to exclaim with the Psalmist, *'I will thank you, Lord, with all my heart; I will tell of all the marvelous things you have done. I will be filled with joy because of you. I will sing praises to your name, O Most High'* *(Psalm 9: 1–2).*

Reflection

The Lord desires that we do not step out before we are whole. Being whole does not mean we are perfect; it means that we have addressed our longings and desires with God, found deep satisfaction with Him and our lives as single women, understood our patterns and made any necessary changes, and become strong in the areas that made us vulnerable to bad relationships. Is there a shift you need to make or a command from the Lord that you need to put into practice that will put you back on His best path? What might that be?

Prayer

God, teach me to wait on You and trust that in Your timing You will satisfy the desires of my heart. In the meantime Lord, help me to recognise the way You are leading me, to give You praise for the blessings in my life right now, and to be busy with the gifts and talents You have placed in my hands.

Receive a new life

*But the Lord still waits for you to come to him so he can show you
his love and compassion. (Isaiah 30: 18)*

My life has never been the same since I accepted Jesus. It is His
will that we all come to know Him and love Him too. He says,
*'You have been chosen to know me, believe in me, and understand
that I alone am God. There is no other God; there never has been
and never will be' (Isaiah 43: 10).*

God wants us to know for ourselves that He is like no one
else we have ever known. Think about His uniqueness for a
moment. The Lord is like no other. This truth challenged my
assumptions about God because I often thought of Him in
terms of my experiences here on earth. I expected Him to
respond the way men have. Yet even amongst the best of men,
there is no one who can outshine the marvellous wonderment
of our awesome Lord. There is simply no one like Him. His
love is altogether wonderful, solid, sure, faithful, never-ending,
permanent, all-consuming, passionate, amazing, loyal, secure,
trustworthy and unconditional!

You were not created to wander aimlessly from one broken
love affair to the next. You have been chosen to know and trust
in the God who is like no other. He is the One who describes
Himself as *'the merciful and gracious God. I am slow to anger and
rich in unfailing love and faithfulness. I show this unfailing love
to many thousands by forgiving every kind of sin and rebellion'
(Exodus 34: 6–7).* God, our Father, showed the extent of His love
when He allowed His only Son, Jesus Christ, to die on the cross
for all our wrongdoings. Our debts have been paid and God
has made peace with us.

Accepting His love and forgiveness requires receiving a new heart, one that is responsive and desires to know Him. Without it, our natural desires will find the things of the world more appealing than knowing Him and any efforts to change will be hampered by our weaknesses and hardheartedness.

A changed heart understands why nothing in this world satisfies for very long. You have the opportunity right now to know this fulfilment. All you need to do is pray a simple, sincere prayer asking Jesus to come into your life and make His home in you. Utter these words from your heart:

Dear Lord,

I am tired of searching for fulfilment. I am tired of hoping each new relationship will reward me with love. I am tired of doing things on my own. I know I have done many wrong things in my life and I am asking for Your forgiveness. I am broken and alone and I need Your comfort. I am weary and in need of love; please fill me with the love I need. I want a new start. Please give me a new heart, one that desires to follow you, for I accept Jesus Christ as my Personal Saviour.

In Jesus name,

Amen

Conclusion

Honey seems tasteless to a person who is full, but even bitter food tastes sweet to the hungry. (Proverbs 27: 7)

As a result of writing a book about relationships, I am often asked if I have found Mr Right. My simple and honest answer is no. Does that mean my journey does not have a happy ending because I am single? Of course not! If my message was about God saving me so that I could gain a husband, I would be selling you a false message about God's ultimate plan for my life. He sought me out to save and set me free from the power of sin, transform my character so I become more and more like His Son, Jesus Christ, and give me the gift of eternal life so that I can always be with Him. This is the same plan He has for each of us.

The Lord has taken my empty heart and satisfied my deepest needs, but I can still remember how different life was when I was hungry for love. I was dragged in all directions, making any relationship seem worth my commitment. Looking for love was a bit like going shopping on an empty stomach, filling my life with things I didn't need and ultimately didn't want. Hunger, whether physical or emotional, can distort our perception and tastes; a bad relationship can taste good to a hungry heart, making us think we would be worse off without it.

This is my happy ending: I am in the right place for love to happen. My motives have changed. I desire companionship rather than hunger for a relationship to satisfy my wounded heart's cry for relief. Though I hope to meet the right person for me, first and foremost I am committed to God's plan for my life *(Ephesians 2: 10)*. It is easy to miss that plan when we are governed by our hurts and stubbornness, so becoming the right person to receive God's best is the most important thing we can do.

Following God's plan does not mean I have no mind of my own and can't make choices. It means I choose to place my trust in God's will; I have finally learned that He is not out to hurt me.

I recently read that we won't be truly satisfied with anything or anyone else until we have found contentment and love with God. As I have tasted God's love I believe this to be true. I now have a deep satisfaction inside and I don't have to play the old game of mentally picking imaginary petals off a flower trying to guess where I stand with our Lord. I know He loves me.

I have loved you, my people, with an everlasting love. With unfailing love I have drawn you to myself. (Jeremiah 31: 3)

Appendices

Basic rights and needs

God is concerned about the rights of those who have been oppressed, controlled and abused and below is an example of the freedoms and rights He desires to reinstate for them.

The Lord gives me freedom...

...to make my own decisions

Each person should have a personal conviction about this matter. *(Romans 14: 5)*

But if you are unwilling to serve the Lord, then choose today whom you will serve. *(Joshua 24: 15)*

...to truthfully express how I feel

But this is what you must do: Tell the truth to each other. *(Zechariah 8: 16)*

...to have space and time for myself

But Jesus often withdrew to the wilderness for prayer. *(Luke 5: 16)*

...to enjoy life and be playful

So go ahead. Eat your food and drink your wine with a happy heart, for God approves of this! Wear fine clothes, with a dash of cologne! *(Ecclesiastes 9: 7–8)*

So I pray that God, who gives you hope, will keep you happy and full of peace as you believe in him. May you overflow with hope through the power of the Holy Spirit. *(Romans 15: 13)*

...to live in a non-abusive environment

Hate what is wrong. Stand on the side of the good. Love each other with genuine affection and take delight in honouring each other. *(Romans 12: 9–10)*

Now I will sing out my thanks to the Lord! Praise the Lord! For though I was poor and needy, he delivered me from my oppressors. *(Jeremiah 20: 13)*

...to develop my skills and talents

A spiritual gift is given to each of us as a means of helping the entire church. *(1 Corinthians 12: 7)*

God has given each of us the ability to do certain things well. *(Romans 12: 6)*

...to appreciate the way God has designed me

Thank you for making me so wonderfully complex! *(Psalm 139: 14)*

...to reason and have my own thoughts and opinions

Though good advice lies deep within a person's heart, the wise will draw it out.. *(Proverbs 20: 5)*

For the Lord grants wisdom! From his mouth come knowledge and understanding. He grants a treasure of good sense to the godly. *(Proverbs 2: 6–7)*

...to protect my children from abuse

The children of your people will live in security. Their children's children will thrive in your presence. *(Psalm 102: 28)*

...to receive forgiveness so I don't keep beating myself up for my weaknesses and sins

Have mercy on me, O God, because of your unfailing love. Because of your great compassion, blot out the stain of my sins. *(Psalm 51: 1)*

For all have sinned; all fall short of God's glorious standard. *(Romans 3: 23)*

...to earn money and be responsible for my finances

She goes out to inspect a field and buys it; with her earnings she plants a vineyard. She is energetic and strong, a hard worker. She watches for bargains; her lights burn late into the night. *(Proverbs 31: 16–18)*

...to recognise I am deeply loved and accepted

God showed how much he loved us by sending his only Son into the world so that we might have eternal life through him. This is real love. It is not that we loved God, but that he loved us and sent his Son as a sacrifice to take away our sin. *(1 John 4: 9–10)*

...to live without fear

Fearing people is a dangerous trap, but to trust the Lord means safety. *(Proverbs 29: 25)*

Fear of the Lord gives life, security, and protection from harm. *(Proverbs 19: 23)*

...to recognise my needs are important to God

Come quickly to help me, O Lord my saviour. *(Psalm 38: 22)*

As for me, I am poor and needy, but the Lord is thinking about me right now. You are my helper and my saviour. Do not delay, O my God. *(Psalm 40: 17)*

'What do you want me to do for you?' Jesus asked. *(Mark 10: 51)*

...to be angry rather than denying it or suppressing it until I explode

Be angry, yet do not sin. Do not let the sun go down on your wrath. *(Ephesians 4: 26 ISV)*

...to build friendships and be safe and comfortable around people

Wounds from a friend are better than many kisses from an enemy. The heartfelt counsel of a friend is as sweet as perfume and incense. *(Proverbs 27: 6, 9)*

The words of the godly lead to life; evil people cover up their harmful intentions. *(Proverbs 10: 11)*

...to change and grow

We will hold to the truth in love, becoming more and more in every way like Christ. *(Ephesians 4: 15)*

...to seek assistance from the police and other care agencies

The authorities are sent by God to help you. *(Romans 13: 4)*

...to set boundaries and say no

If another believer sins against you, go privately and point out the fault. If the other person listens and confesses it, you have won that person back. *(Matthew 18: 15; see also vv. 16–19)*

I will not allow deceivers to serve in my house and liars will not serve in my presence *(See Psalm 101).*

Healthy relationships

Healthy relationships are built by people who accept themselves, take responsibility for their individual happiness and personal growth, express their feelings truthfully, and enforce personal boundaries. These individuals gravitate towards and attract similar types of people with which to build relationships.

Healthy relationships begin with mutual attraction, interests, and chemistry, but grow patiently and steadily while compatibility and common goals are explored. These relationships are bonded by commitment, care, respect, a willingness to work out problems, and a desire to work on building a life together.

Within these relationships you will find:

- A desire to share open and honest communication
- Respect for each other's opinions and needs
- A safe and supportive environment in which each person is free to be him or herself
- Effort made to work out conflicts fairly
- Individual responsibility and accountability for growth and change
- Trust in each other's autonomy, individual friendships, goals, and interests
- Shared responsibility and parenting
- Both partners benefiting from financial arrangements
- Decision making as a team
- Both partners providing love, support, and appreciation
- Humour and fun

Unhealthy relationships

Unhealthy relationships are developed by wounded people who are hoping another person will fix their brokenness. These relationships are intense and tend to develop very quickly. Commitments to the future of the relationship start early in the dating process and decisions are based on feelings rather than the reality of who each person is. Boundaries that define an individual's identity and needs are compromised, breached, or neglected through fear of losing the relationship.

What is domestic abuse?

Domestic abuse is a pattern of aggressive or controlling behaviours carried out within the context of an intimate relationship. These behaviours can involve sexual, physical, financial, or emotional abuse and can happen to anybody regardless of sexual preference, race, culture, age, lifestyle, or class. It is more commonly instigated by a man towards a woman. Domestic abuse includes both threats and actual instances of physical violence.

Why is he abusive?

An abuser's behaviour stems from his values and beliefs about intimate relationships. He believes that he is entitled to certain privileges that do not apply to his partner. He sees her as a possession rather than an equal and exercises abuse in order to gain power and control over her.

Types of abuse*

Financial – taking money from you, making you ask for money, giving you an allowance, stopping you from working or from keeping a job

Emotional – playing mind games, putting you down, calling you names, and making you feel bad about yourself

Sexual – treating you as a sexual object, forcing you to have sex, doing sexual things against your wishes, attacking sexual parts of your body

Physical – hitting, slapping, pushing, punching, biting, twisting arms, using weapons, grabbing, beating, choking

Isolation – controlling what you do, where you go, and who you see and talk to

Using male privilege – treating you like a servant, making all the 'big' decisions

Intimidation – making and carrying out threats, throwing objects, threatening to commit suicide, hurting/injuring animals, threatening to take children

Using children – using children to cause guilt, giving messages to children, turning children against you, using visitation rights to harass you

Spiritual abuse – using God/scripture to control and use you, using spiritual authority to control and manipulate you

* Power and control wheel (adapted)

www.theduluthmodel.org

Some of the early warning signs?

- Too much too soon. He pushes for closeness and does not allow you to go at a pace that is comfortable for you

- Changes expectations or guidelines so that you are left feeling confused as to how to please him

- He puts down and speaks disrespectfully of former partners and/or has a negative attitude towards women.

- He is disrespectful to you and ignores, makes light of, or belittles your complaints.

- He is controlling/ jealous/ possessive, constantly checks up on you, and/or insists you spend all your free time together.

- He is prone to anger, unpredictable behaviour, mood swings, anger out of proportion for incident

- He never sees anything as his fault and blames you for the way he behaves

- He pressures you to do things or give up important values to meet his wishes and demands

- He is focused on his needs and preferences and ignores your wishes

- He is an addict

- He has a history of abusing women, violence, and/or criminal activity

- He has one set of standards for himself and another for you

If any of the above attitudes or behaviours makes you feel uncomfortable, let him know as soon as possible which ones are unacceptable to you. If he continues, make it clear that the relationship cannot go forward until the attitude or behaviour is addressed. If he still continues or resorts to another inappropriate behaviour, this is a sign that he is not ready to own his problem and be committed to a path of change and growth.

What should I do if my relationship is abusive?

- Speak to a national domestic violence agency that can offer you information about your options
- Break free from isolation and shame by speaking to someone who can understand what is happening to you
- Find safe, supportive people who won't say things to make you feel as if the abuse is your fault
- Find out if your church has a domestic violence policy and/or people who can pray for and support you
- Learn about the abuse mentality, what domestic violence is, and the warning signs to look for so you can identify what is happening to you and avoid blaming yourself
- Find a counsellor who understands the abuse mentality, its affects and who can offer you the right kind of support
- Take time out for yourself so you can think and take care of your needs
- Bring your life under God's love and protection, asking Him to make a way for you. He will set you free from abusive relationships and the cycle of loving men who love poorly in return

The Right Step Relationship Course

Joanne has designed 'The Right Step Relationship Course – a series of 12 workshops that assist women in developing essential relationship skills, including how to break unhealthy relationship patterns and be free to build healthier relationships.

If you would like to attend/arrange a speaking engagement or workshop at your church/organisation, please contact Joanne Robinson through her website *www.donnaintera.co.uk* or *www.loveinseason.net*

Feedback from workshop participants

'It was a great help. I wish I could have attended these workshops 30 years ago'.

'I no longer find that I am second guessing myself. When I date I just enjoy the date without worrying what he is thinking'.

'I find I am able to say no and set boundaries'.

'I liked the way we could discuss issues freely, be honest if we didn't understand and be accepted for our views'

'I loved the information, so rarely available!'

'We got to address areas of women's lives that we struggle with through lack of understanding.'

'I would like to say thank you so much. I had the courage to end a bad relationship because of your course.'

'The Domestic Violence part of the course was hard to hear but I really needed to hear it. It has been really helpful, thank you.'

'The course gave me hope in my future relationships. There can be change.'